Physical Characteristics of the Pointer

(from the American Kennel Club breed standard)

Back: Strong and solid with only a slight rise from croup to top of shoulders. Loin of moderate length, powerful and slightly arched. Croup falling only slightly to base of tail. Tuck-up should be apparent, but not exaggerated.

Tail: Heavier at the root, tapering to a fine point. Length no greater than to hock.

Hindquarters: Muscular and powerful with great propelling leverage. Thighs long and well developed. Stifles well bent. The hocks clean; the legs straight as viewed from behind.

Size: *Dogs: Height—25–28 inches, Weight—55–75 pounds. Bitches: Height—23–26 inches, Weight—44–65 pounds.*

Color: Liver, lemon, black, orange; either in combination with white or solid-colored. In the darker colors, the nose should be black or brown; in the lighter shades it may be lighter or flesh-colored.

Pointer

◇

By Richard G. Beauchamp

Contents

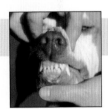

KENNEL CLUB BOOKS® POINTER
ISBN: 1-59378-266-7

Copyright © 2006 • Kennel Club Books, LLC
308 Main Street, Allenhurst, NJ 07711 USA
Cover Design Patented: US 6,435,559 B2 • Printed in South Korea

Photography by Carol Ann Johnson and Michael Trafford
with additional photographs by:

John Ashbey, Rich Bergman, Paulette Braun, Carolina Biological Supply, Isabelle Français, Gilbert Studios, Graham Studios, Bill Jonas, Dr. Dennis Kunkel, Tam C. Nguyen, Phototake, Jean Claude Revy, Philippe Roca and Missy Yuhl.

Illustrations by Renée Low and Patricia Peters.

The publisher wishes to thank all of the owners whose dogs are illustrated in this book, including Erica and John Bandes, Barbara Cherry and Wendy Gordon.

Special thanks to Wayne Cavanaugh, Nona Kilgore Bauer and Philippe Roca for their assistance with this book.

Countries throughout Europe have developed their own versions of "pointing dogs," but the breed that bears the name Pointer is the one hailing from England, shown here.

POINTER

In *The Natural History of Dogs*, a fascinating and enlightening study of the development of the dog breeds of the world, authors Richard and Alice Feinnes classify most dogs as having descended from one of four major groups, all of which trace back to separate and distinct branches of the wolf family. These four classifications are the Dingo Group, the Greyhound Group, the Northern Group and the Mastiff Group. It is important to have at least a basic understanding of these groups, as very few breeds of dog are of pure descent; instead, they owe their widely diverse characteristics to an intermingling of the blood of as many as all four of the groups.

The Pointer, whose ancestors are many and greatly varied, today possesses a purity and nobility that are all his own.

FROM HIS ANCESTORS...

It is believed that the solid-colored Pointers are the result of the cross that was made to the Greyhound many generations ago. On occasion, solid-color black, liver and, more rarely, orange and lemon Pointers may be seen. The highly developed eyesight of the Pointer can easily be attributed to the breed's sighthound ancestor, as can a Pointer's aloof and aristocratic demeanor.

The Dingo Group traces its origin to the Asian wolf (*Canis lupus pallipes*). Two well-known examples of the Dingo Group are the Basenji and, through the crossing of several European breeds, the Rhodesian Ridgeback.

The Greyhound Group descends from a coursing-type relative of the Asian wolf. The group includes all those dogs that hunt by sight and are capable of great speed. The Greyhound itself, the Afghan Hound, the Borzoi and the Irish Wolfhound are all examples of this group. These dogs also are known as the coursing breeds or sighthounds, though they are not true hounds, as they do not

The Italian Pointer is known as the Bracco Italiano, colored in chestnut, orange and/or white.

hunt by scent. It is worth noting that the Pointer has been influenced by this group of swift-moving hunters.

The Arctic or Nordic (Northern) Group of dogs is a direct descendant of the rugged northern wolf (*Canis lupus*). Included in this group are the Alaskan Malamute, Chow Chow, German Shepherd and the much smaller spitz-type dogs.

The fourth classification, and the one that is of special interest to those who wish to research the history of the Pointer, is the Mastiff Group. This group owes its primary heritage to the Tibetan wolf (*Canis lupus chanco* or *laniger*). The great diversity of dogs included in this group indicates that they are not entirely of pure origins, as they have undoubtedly been influenced by descendants of the other three groups.

The widely divergent descendants of the Mastiff Group are known to include many of the scenting breeds—breeds that find game by the use of their olfactory senses rather than by sight. These breeds include those we now classify as gundogs and the true hounds.

As man became more sophisticated and his lifestyle more complex, he found that he could produce dogs that could suit his specific needs from the various descendants of the wolf. Often these needs were based on the manner in which man himself went after game on particular terrain. The importance here is that man had taken control of the individual dogs that mated. Specific characteristics were prized, and inbreeding

The Perdiguero de Burgos stands between 20 and 24 inches tall and weighs up to 66 pounds. He is known as the Spanish Pointer.

The Braque du Bourbonnais, in brown, liver or orange roan, is also known as the Bourbonnais Pointer, a handsome French hunting dog.

The Braque d'Auvergne, one of the many pointers of France, stands 24 inches high and is marked in a black and white roaning pattern.

practices were employed to perpetuate these characteristics.

One type of hunting dog that man developed retained the wolf characteristics of pursuing the prey until it was cornered and killed or chased up a tree. This practice is more or less typical of that group of dogs known today as our scenthounds. While their tenacity was held in high regard, the hounds' willingness to continue the chase for miles, if necessary, often became rather tiresome for their owners. Thus was born a need for the hunting dog that never followed through with the chase or the

attack. The dog's job was not to do the hunting or killing but rather to assist the human hunter by finding the game and indicating his discovery to the hunter quietly so as not to scare away the birds. Furthermore, like any good assistant, the dog obeyed his master's commands without hesitation.

References have been made to the existence of this kind of dog as early as the time of the ancient Greeks. Written records point to the existence of a rough-coated breed of dog in Italy that signaled his discovery of game to the hunter by assuming a rigid position and placing his body in direct line with the find.

Today we think of the Pointer as a distinct breed of dog, but in fact the name refers to a dog that works the field in a distinctive manner, not unlike that described in ancient Greece. Countries throughout Europe developed their own unique breeds of "pointers" or "pointing dogs" based upon the

A well-balanced pointing dog, the Braque Saint-Germain derived from the Pointer and is characteristically colored in orange and white.

However, many of Britain's Pointer aficionados beg to differ.

The Pointer and His Predecessors, written by William Arkwright of Sutton Scarsdale, near Chesterfield, England, is the most universally accepted work on the development of the Pointer breed. He began work on his book late in the 19th century and researched the material included over a period of

A photograph from the turn of the 19th century, showing trained Pointers in the field. The photo was captioned "Waiting the Flight."

demands made by their specific terrain. The results of these efforts can be seen in Italy's Bracco Italiano and Spinone Italiano, Germany's Shorthaired and Wirehaired Pointers, the Braque Francais and Brittany of France, as well as Britain's contribution, the breed known simply as the Pointer.

Popular but controversial opinion has influenced many to believe that all of the pointing breeds owe their basic foundation to Spain and that the Pointer, as developed in Great Britain, owes its source exclusively to the Spanish Pointer, the Perdiguero de Burgos.

Drayton Lady and Eng. Ch. Coronation, a brace of show and working Pointer bitches owned by Mr. H. Sawtell, circa 1935.

POINTERS ON THE CONTINENT

Every major European nation has produced its own version of the Pointer, with Germany and France leading the list. France has nine such breeds, including the multi-talented Brittany, Wirehaired Pointing Griffon, also called Korthals Griffon, and the seven Braques named for their regions, such as the Auvergne, Bourbonnais and Saint-Germain. Germany has six distinct pointing breeds, including the Stichelhaar, Weimaraner, Pudelpointer and the German Short-, Wire- and Longhaired Pointers.

Hungary boasts its talented Vizsla; Slovakia its Cesky Fousek; the Slavs their incredibly popular Dalmatian; Italy its Bracco Italiano and Segugio Italiano, both gaining fans in the UK; Spain its Perdiguero de Burgos and Navarro; and Portugal its Perdigueiro Portugueso. Belgium's Shorthaired Pointer is considered extremely rare, as are the two Danish breeds, the Old Danish Bird Dog (or *Gammel Dansk Hønsehund*) and the Hertha Pointer.

ADAPTABILITY AND SOPHISTICATION

Hunting has demanded different skills through the ages, and the dogs that man has used in this pursuit have also changed. In the earliest stages, man hunted to obtain food and to get rid of dangerous beasts. As man developed his techniques, and hunting began to be regulated by the government, it became a sporting event and the duties of his dogs became increasingly complex. Those who fancy the Pointer as a hunter believe that their breed represents the highest level of canine adaptability and sophistication.

30 years. Throughout this work, Arkwright, while fully admitting the existence of a Spanish Pointer in England, maintained that the influence of the Spanish dog had little, if any, effect on the development of his chosen breed.

Lending credence to Arkwright's belief is *Anecdotes of Dogs*, written by Edward Jesse, Esq., and published in 1880. Jesse wrote of the Spanish Pointer in England during his day and describes a dog so unlike the Pointer as we know it that it is difficult to associate the two breeds. "How well do I recollect in my early youth seeing the slow, heavy, solemn-looking, and thick-shouldered (*sic*) Spanish pointer, tired with two or three hours' work

in turnips, and so stiff after it the next day, as to be little capable of resuming his labors."

Although he does go on to explain away the streamlining of the breed by a simple cross to the "fox-hound," certainly one would question whether the so-called fox-hound of that era had the conformation that would produce the lithe lines and increased speed of the Pointer as we know it. Arkwright not only dismisses the Spanish dog as the foundation of the Pointer, he also casts doubt on Spain as the origin of the pointing breeds in the first place. He refers to a letter written by the US Vice Consul in Valencia, Spain in 1900. In that letter the Vice Consul stated

In 1895 this rare black bitch, Leader, made a name for herself in the field. She belonged to breed expert William Arkwright.

The famous Lloyd Price's Pointer, named Wragg. This painting was published in 1881 and is an interesting comparison to the Pointers of today.

Sandford Dum Dum is an example of an old-time Pointer, produced from Foxhound and Spanish Pointer breeding.

Tilleman painting of the Duke of Kingston with his kennel of Pointers in 1725. Drury describes these dogs as "…the same elegant Franco-Italian type as the pointing dogs painted by Oudry (1686–1755) and Desportes (1661–1743) at the end of the 17th century."

Finally, and contrary to what has been readily accepted by many theorists, research indicates that the pointing dog was well established in France long before the Spanish Pointer made its way to Great Britain. Moreover, those French dogs, very frequently seen

that pointing dogs existed in Spain for many generations and were the descendants of an original pair that were presented as gifts to the Spanish court "by an Italian prince."

Colonel David Hancock has researched this question of origin quite thoroughly in his excellent work *The Heritage of the Dog,* and the Drury book *British Dogs* revealed that the first record of the Pointer in Great Britain is the

> ## DOG SHOW CONQUERED
> England's prestigious Crufts Dog Show has been conquered by the Pointer on two occasions, the first of which was in 1935 by Pennine Prima Donna, owned by A. Eggleston, and the second in 1958 by Eng. Ch. Chiming Bells, owned by Mrs. W. Parkinson.

throughout Great Britain, far more closely resembled the Pointer of today than the Spanish dogs.

OTHER INFLUENCES

"Horses for courses" is an old saying among British stockmen that has served as the basis for the development of many kinds of prized livestock. Translated in layman's terms, this adage simply refers to choosing a breeding formula that will produce a horse best suited to work in the terrain of

Eng. Ch. Flagon of Ardagh was a top winner of the late 1920s/early 1930s. He added to his many honors two further Challenge Certificates in 1933, at the age of seven.

This original painting of a Spanish Pointer by renowned dog artist Reinagle appeared in *The Sportsman's Cabinet* in 1803.

the region. This formula not only applied to horses but also was the basis upon which many of Britain's outstanding dog breeds were developed. Often this practice required going to totally unrelated breeds for what was needed. At times a dash of one breed, a smattering of another and perhaps even a sprinkling of two or three others were necessary to complete the recipe for the ideal dog! Although this practice was not particularly something to be shouted from the rooftops, it is to what we owe the incredible characteristics of some of our modern-day breeds, including the Pointer.

Perhaps the question of the Pointer's country of origin will never be satisfactorily answered, but there is no doubt that the gene pool of its descendants is certainly diverse. Breed historians acknowledge that at least four crosses to other breeds were employed to bring about the Pointer as we know it today. The four breeds credited are the Greyhound, the Bloodhound, the Foxhound and, more surprisingly, the Bull Terrier.

At first reading, these crosses may seem to be somewhat bizarre choices. However, you will see how these crosses made perfect sense in our forefathers' attempt to produce the ideal hunting dog. You will also see that these astute breeders had to take a bit of the bitter for the sake of the sweet. There are a number of problems resulting from these crosses that continue to haunt the breed today, many generations later.

This photo, circa 1930, was captioned "Pointers at School on the Moors."

Nancolleth Billy Mischief was the name of this dog bred by Mrs. F. A. Rowe in 1931.

Rock of Ballymoy, a Pointer of the 1930s, was bred by Mr. G. Davies and owned by Mrs. M. V. Christian.

His Grace the Duke of Montrose was a renowned Pointer expert who owned one of the most important kennels in the breed. Two Pointers of his breeding are shown (foreground) in this photo taken at the 1930 Ulster Gun Trials.

REMARKABLE!

One of the most remarkable Pointers in the breed's history was the dog Drake, who had been bred by Sir R. Garth and sold by him at what was then considered a "staggering figure" to Mr. R. J. Lloyd Price of Wales. The dog was then at the advanced age of seven years but was said to work the field far better than even puppies of the highest class. The speed at which he worked was such that he sent up a cloud of dust when he stopped to drop to the scent of game.

Let us look first at the Greyhound cross. There can be no doubt that the use of Greyhound blood gave the modern Pointer its speed, elegance and grace. The short sleek coat harkens back to the breed's Greyhound ancestor, as does the long, well-arched neck, graceful underline and turn-on-the-spot agility. On the other hand, the Greyhound cross can plague the breeder with excessive refinement of head. A narrow front and rib cage, a tilted pelvis and excessive loin arch are also undesirable characteristics that sometimes appear in the Pointer.

The Pointer is not alone in its use of the ancient Bloodhound for its highly developed scenting ability and robust constitution. The undesirable features that accompanied those highly desirable Bloodhound characteristics, however, were the plodding movement, long rounded ears and straight underline, with which Pointer breeders are still forced to contend.

Foxhound blood was also incorporated for scenting ability and easy maintenance. The well-developed rib cage and relentless endurance were positive assets as well. Such advantages were not without their price, however, as round bone, plain heads, long ropy tails carried vertically and houndy underlines plague the breed to this day.

There are probably few breeds more alert or persistent and determined than the Bull Terrier, and this is what the early Pointer breeders sought. However, the barrel chest, the overly broad front and the hard-bitten terrier eye and expression were contributions the Pointer did not need.

Despite such problems, the Pointer breed rapidly took shape, and the future of the breed was certainly given a major boost in the right direction by the aristocratic names who took up the breed: Lord Lichfield, the Duke of Kingston, Lord Mexborough and the Earl of Lauderdale, just to name a few.

Four early dogs are generally given credit for laying the foundation for all that was to come in the breed: Brocton's Bounce, Stater's Major, Whitehouse's Hamlet and Garth's Drake (who was said to be one-eighth Foxhound) were the names that dominated Pointer circles. Eng. Ch. Ranger, a dog

Stainton Startler was born in 1932 and won his first Challenge Certificate in 1933 at the Scottish Kennel Club Show.

Pennine Prima Donna, born in 1931, is not considered a champion despite having won 12 Challenge Certificates and even Best in Show (BIS) at Crufts.

owned by Mr. Newton, became the breed's first bench champion, winning three first prizes at England's premier events—Leeds and Birmingham in 1861, and the final award at Chelsea in 1863. Eng. Ch. Flash gained her title at Birmingham in 1865. The first field trial champion was Drake, born in 1868, bred and owned by Sir Richard Garth. Henry Sawtell bred and owned the breed's first Dual Champion, Faskally Brag, who was also a sire of significant impact.

In the end, British stockmanship produced an elegant animal, strikingly painted and blessed with exquisite balance and proportion. Of crucial importance was his

Jake's Carolina Boy, an American-bred Pointer of the 1930s. He was owned by Miss Claudia Lea Phelps and won the Amateur Derby Stakes, held by the Pinehurst Field Trials Club in Pinehurst, North Carolina.

unmatched ability to perform in the field. Here was a tenacious hunter willing to meet the demands of any job assigned to him. Descriptions such as "a paragon of the pointing breeds" and "a non-stop hunting machine" reverberated throughout the hillsides, sounding loud and clear across the English Channel to the rest of Europe and then across the Atlantic to America.

POINTERS IN THE UNITED STATES

English settlers coming to America, a country overflowing in game and open land, no doubt brought their superb hunting dogs with them, thus the beginning of the Pointer in America can be traced to pre-Colonial times. The first documented importations of Pointers began in the late 1870s, notably those of the newly formed Westminster Kennel Club, including their trademark dog Sensation, and the St. Louis Kennel Club, which imported a fast field dog named Sleaford in 1877. The famed Westminster Pointer, as

history would have it, hardly lived up to his namesake: as a matter of fact, his "unsensational" show record reflects that he won his championship entirely under Westminster judges and was sold at auction for $35, not an impressive sum even back then. Some other famous imports of this period were: Bow, imported by T.H. Scott; Meteor, the first small Pointer who excelled as a stud dog, imported by the St. Louis Kennel Club; Faust, imported by S.A. Kaye; and Croxteth, brought over by Rev. J.C. MacDonna in 1879 and sold to Mr. Dodeffroy of New York. This young

WESTMINSTER COAT OF ARMS

The Pointer became the symbol of the nation's most prestigious dog show, the Westminster Kennel Club show. The club's first English import, "Sensation," is used as the club's logo. The Pointer took the honor of Best in Show at that show three times during the 20th century. The first Pointer to win Westminster was R.F. Maloney's Int. Ch. Governor Moscow in 1925. The second of these victories was claimed by Ch. Nancolleth Markable, owned by the famous Giralda Farms, in 1932. Over 50 years later, in 1986, Ch. Marjetta National Acclaim, owned by Mrs. A.R. Robson and Michael Zollo, won Best in Show at Madison Square Garden in New York City, the third and last Pointer to win Westminster in the century.

dog improved the quality of American Pointers, being a better size and shape than the dogs in the States, with stronger bone, more muscle and a long, lean head, different from the cloddy heads imported by the others.

Arnold Burges's *The American Kennel and Sporting Field* was published in 1876, and the National American Kennel Club followed, along with Dr. N. Rowe's *American Kennel Stud Book*. The first pointing-dog field trial, sponsored by the Tennessee State Sportsmen's Association, was held in October 1874 near Memphis, Tennessee. A black and white Pointer named Rex, owned by A. Merriman, came in sixth place, scoring 67 out of a possible 100 points.

The very first Pointer to be registered by the American Kennel Club (AKC) was a black and white dog by the name of Ace of Spades, even though this dog was by no means one of the first dogs imported into the country. Whelped in June 1875, Ace was owned by J.J. Snellenberg of New Brighton, Pennsylvania. He was sired by Button, who was out of David Stewart's brace imported from Britain.

Edmund Orgill of New York, who greatly favored the lemon and white dogs, bred and owned many famous Pointers in this period, including Ch. Orgill's Rush, born in April 1876, as well as Beulah, Rap,

Ch. Shandown's Touch O'Kings, BIS at Forsyth KC in 1972, handled by Bobby Barlow under judge Mrs. John B. Patterson.

Rose and Ruby. In September 1882, Don, owned by R.T. Vandevort, made Pointer history by winning first place in the Free-For-All stake of the National American Kennel Club's trials in Minnesota.

Imports continued from England in the 1880s with the arrival of Eng. Ch. Graphic and Nell of Efford, imported by Mr. James L. Anthony of New York in 1885. These dogs owned by Mr. Norrish came from Devonshire, England. They proved top winning dogs and valuable breeding stock.

A group of the most important Pointer men in the US banded together to create the Pointer Club of America to safeguard the breed: among the members in 1890 were Hon. John S. Wise, president; George W. LaRue, secretary and treasurer; and James L. Anthony, first of four vice-presidents. Artist

Ch. Cumbrian Black Pearl, winning a Group at Santa Barbara KC in 1983, handled by Corky Vroom. The following year Black Pearl was the number-one Sporting Dog and the top Pointer of all time.

Gustav Muss-Arnolt was the Pointer Club of America's first AKC delegate.

In 1889 the black and white dog Rip Rap came on the scene to distinguish himself in field trials. This color was not desirable by American fanciers at the time, but Rip Rap changed their minds. He sired 19 field trial winners, including Young Rip Rap, a famous producer and show dog. Ripsey, sired by Rip Rap, became the most famous dog of Edmund Osthaus's kennel, one of the leading field Pointer breeding establishments for decades.

James Monroe Avent and Hobart Ames founded the National Bird Dog Championship in West Point, Mississippi in 1896. Bird dog trialers consider this the most important of all trials, though it wasn't won by a Pointer until 1909,

when the three-year-old Manitoba Rap, bred by W.T.F. Fielde and owned by Thomas Johnson, did so. In 1915 the 6,000-acre Ames Plantation became the event's permanent home where the trial is still conducted. Among the Pointers who have dominated the trial, three of the early multiple national winners were bitches: Mary Montrose, four-time winner; Becky Broomhill, three-time winner; and Mary Blue, two-time winner. Other multiple winners over the decades were Ariel, Paladin, Palamonium, and Whipporwill's Rebel.

On November 14, 1900, the Pointer Club of America held its inaugural field trial at Jamesport, Long Island, New York. FC Alford's John and Fishel's Frank appeared on the scene in the early 1900s and upped the ante for the breed in field trials. Frank sired 58 field trial winners, including "Peerless" Mary Montrose, the four-time national winner and Winners Bitch at the 1917 Westminster show, Comanche Frank and John Proctor, the latter two going back to Alford's John. All of these dogs won nationals and established major lines in Pointers in the US.

A number of important show dogs emerged in the 1920s and 1930s, including Ch. Governor Moscow, the 1925 Westminster Best in Show (BIS) winner, as well as Ch. Nancolleth Belle and Ch. Dapple Joe, both Westminster Group winners. The next Pointer

AMERICAN POINTER CLUB

The breed's current AKC parent club is the American Pointer Club, Inc. (APC), which was established in 1938. The APC acts as the guardian and promoter of the breed in the US. One of its main goals is to protect the breed standard and encourage its members to breed to it. Another important goal is promoting the versatility of the Pointer breed. The club does this in many ways, including sponsoring agility, obedience, field trials and hunting tests in conjunction with the APC's national specialty. Further, the club created the Versatility program to award Pointers who achieve excellence in multiple areas of competition (conformation, agility, field, tracking and hunting tests). The VA (Versatility Award) and the VAX (Versatility Award Excellent) are the titles earned through the program.

establishing a whole line of exquisite, intelligent Pointers. No Pointer expert would dispute that the Elhew line dominated the field for the last half of the 20th century, so much so that many Pointer folk refer to the "Elhew Pointer" as if it were a separate breed or model. Although Bob concentrated on field dogs, he was proud to maintain conformation in his line and on the rare occasion would show one of his "good-looking" Elhew dogs in the ring with success. To this day, the Elhew dogs are a force in the breed; the breeding programs of Rick and Suzanne Glover, the Yellow Rose kennels and others continue to concentrate on these dogs.

The most important Best in Show winner from this period is no doubt Ch. Nancolleth Beryl of Giralda, whose record of 21 BIS awards was not surpassed for nearly five decades, when Ch.

Ch. St. Aldwyns Radiance, BOB at Westminster in 1974, handled by Jeffrey Lynn Brucker.

Westminster BIS winner was Nancolleth Markable, bred by Mrs. F.A. Rowe, who took the title in 1932. Other Westminster Group winners of this period were Ch. Benson of Crombie (1934) and Ch. Nancolleth Marquis (1935).

The Elhew kennels of Bob Wehle were established in 1936, based on Gem of Fearn, a Scottish import, and Frank of Sunnylawn. The foundation of this kennel was Elhew Midge, who has been called "the Lamborghini of Pointers,"

Cumbrian Black Pearl overtook the record in 1984. Another great dog was Int. Ch. Drumgannon Dreadnaught, the sire of 19 champions and a Best in Show winner in the US and England.

The American Pointer Club (APC) became a member of the AKC in 1938 and held its first show in conjunction with the famous Morris and Essex Show in May of the follow year. The winner of the show was a lemon and white dog named Int. Ch. Pennine Paramount of Prune's Own, born in 1935, sired by Marlais Marksman, the most influential Pointer of the 1930s, who had as many fans as he had detractors. Some believe that he

was too houndy with a down face, and he passed these qualities (and many good ones) to his progeny.

The 1950s saw the prominence of Mary Wadsworth Rich's Vilmar kennels, as Ch. Vilmar's Lucky, living up to his name, won the national specialty 5 times, not to mention 12 Best in Show awards. The first orange champion was also a Vilmar dog, Ch. Vilmar's Skogis Herta. Two other greats from the 1950s, both Westminster Group winners, were Ch. C P and Ch. Captain Speck, Lucky's sire. In 1954, five Pointers were inducted into the Field Trial Hall of Fame, which is a part of the National Bird Dog Museum located in Grand Junction, Tennessee. The five dogs were Fishel's Frank, John Proctor, Luminary, Mary Montrose and Muscle Shoal's Jake.

The decade of the 1960s brought forth Ch. Maryjay's Majesty, owned by Enos Phillips. He was a liver and white who won 13 BIS, 2 Bests in Specialty Show (BISS) awards and 61 Group Ones, including the APC's national in 1963 and 1964. Bob Parkers's Truewithem bloodlines relied heavily on his prepotency. Another great Pointer of the period was Ch. Crookrise Danny of Muick, who won Group One at Westminster in 1964.

The Cumbrian kennels were founded in 1967 by Henri Tuthill, basing his line on his first champion, Ch. Shandown's Prima Donna, and English imports such as

Ch. Cumbrian President and Ch. Sunset of Cumbrian. Cumbrian's dedication to the breed has paid off richly, in producing nearly 100 champions including the all-time top-winning Pointer Ch. Cumbrian Black Pearl in the 1980s.

The top Sporting Dog for 1970 was a Pointer by the name of Ch. Counterpoint's Lord Ashley, whose record of 20 Bests in Show by a *male* Pointer has not been overtaken. Lord Ashley was bred by Ruth Still. Among his impressive wins were the APC national in 1965 and 1966 and the Group at Westminster twice. The decades of the 1970s and 80s saw many great accomplishments in the show ring and a historic first in 1978 when the first Dual Champion Pointer, excelling in field and conformation, was achieved: DC Scanpoint's Touch of Troll, owned by Karin B. Ashe. Few could ever imagine going beyond a dual championship title, though DC/AFC Scanpoint's MacKenzie did just that when, in 1984, he became the first Dual Champion Pointer to earn the Amateur Field Champion title. He was trained in the field by Steven Ashe and handled by Karin and Kristen Ashe.

The Marjetta kennels of Marjorie Martorella made a name in Pointers beginning in the 1970s. Marjorie bred her first Pointer litter in 1974 and over the past three decades has produced over 100 champions. Marjorie's foundation dam, Ch. Truewithem A Taste of Triumph, sired by Ch. Counterpoint's Lord Ashley, produced 4 BIS winners among her 29 champions: Ch. Marjetta Lord Carlton, Ch. Marjetta Lady Vanessa, Ch. Marjetta Mylestone and Ch. Marjetta National Acclaim, the 1985 Westminster victor, handled by Michael Zollo and owned by Mrs. Alan Robson. The Marjetta Pointers have been used as the foundation of many current kennels, including Birnamwood, Homestead, Karolina, Kingscroft, Olympus, Steinhoff and Sunset.

Coming into prominence in the early 1970s, the Shandown Pointers of Shan and Leon Shiver owned and produced many top Pointers; among them were Ch. Shandown's King's Ransom, Ch. Shandown's Playboy, Ch. Shandown's King of The Road, Ch. Shandown's Dress Parade, Ch. Shandown's Black Knight, Ch. Shandown's Touch O'Kings and Ch. Shandown's Diamond Jim.

Ch. Marjetta National Acclaim, Best in Show at Westminster in 1986, with handler Michael Zollo.

MORE THAN COMPARING LEMONS AND ORANGES
by Wayne Cavanaugh

In 1979 the very first Pointer with black pigment (a black nose and eye rims) to win the national specialty was Henri Tuthill's orange and white Ch. Cumbrian Sea Breeze. He was 100% English breeding out of an imported dam and by an imported sire. Joyce and Athos Nilson had imported his sire, and Henri had imported his dam from George Holliday, who had obtained her from Peter Woodford at the Stonethorpe kennel. So after 40 consecutive years of liver-nosed national winners, Sea Breeze finally turned the tide.

Prior to this historic win, no Pointer had ever won the national, or even the breed at Westminster, that didn't have liver nose and eye pigment; that is, they were all either livers or lemons. It is generally accepted worldwide that yellow-marked Pointers with liver eye and nose pigment are called "lemons," and yellow-marked pointers with black noses are called "orange" regardless of the shade of yellow, which can be anything from deep bronze to pale buckskin. The reason for this is simple: they produce very different colors when bred—no black nose, no black puppies. Actually with the exception of a few superb imports in the late 1960s and early '70s (a few Crookrise, Toberdoney and Cumbrian dogs from England, and later some from Scandinavia), oranges with black noses and black and white Pointers simply were not even seen in the show ring. That is, they were all liver and white, or the occasional recessive lemon and white, neither of which can carry for black!

The very next year, in 1980, another orange and white won the national, Ch. Rossenarra Amontillado of Crookrise, an orange and white English import. "Myles," as he was known, was only bred to 7 times, due in part perhaps to his then "rare" color, but produced 22 champions, including 3 Best in Show winners—2 blacks and one orange—and still remains on the top sire list. Of the top 13 sires of all time, 6 are his descendants. Perhaps as important, 14 of the last 20 national Best of Breed winners are his descendants. Myles was tightly line-bred on Ch. Crookrise Flint of Kitty Edmonson's old Crookrise line.

Ch. Marjetta National Acclaim, a liver and white, was a Best in Show winner at Westminster. "Deputy," as he was known, was a line-bred dog of the old Truewithem line of the late Bob Parkers. Interestingly, he had a cross to one of those first wave of orange and white imports, Ch. Crookrise Jesse, through his sire's side. Deputy was a hugely popular stud dog, sire of 107 champions, and also remains on the top of the top sire list in the number-one spot. Of the top 13 sires of all time, 3 are his descendants. While he never won the national specialty, 8 of the last 20 national Best of Breed winners were descendants of his; amazingly, all 8 are also descendants of Myles.

The year 1974 marks a special occasion for the Crookrise kennels of England and their dedicated breeders Walter and Kitty Edmonson. At the 1974 national show, Ch. Crookrise Greg won Best of Breed, the first time this kennel won the American national since their inception in the early 1900s. Another Crookrise dog won the national in 1980, this being Ch. Rossenarra Amontillado of Crookrise. Even though the kennel has not produced a top-winning dog in its history, being a small operation, the Crookrise dogs can be found in all but one of the dogs that have won the national specialty in the past 25 years. While the breed no longer has as many large gene pool families as it did in the past, there are few top-winning Pointers in the American show ring today that don't have some variation of the old Crookrise-Truewithem (or a similar English-American cross). This long-standing kennel is continued on by the Edmondsons' daughter, Cicely Robertshaw.

Sally Barton started her Coralwood kennels in 1977. Her acquisition of foundation sire and dam Ch. Sydmar Coralwoods Grand Slam and Ch. Sydmar the Heartless Wench from Paul Nykiel formed the basis of her current breeding line. She has produced many Best in Show Pointers, including Am./Can. Ch. Coralwood-Ash Hollows Bronx

Ch. Woolmen's Apricot Li' l Tipaway, BOB at Santa Barbara KC in 1982, handled by Bobby Barlow.

Bomber, Ch. Coralwood-Ash Hollows Wild Indian, Ch. Coralwood-Troon Leads The League and Ch. Coralwood Fielder's Choice. One of the top dogs bred by Sally came in 1996, in Ch. Oncore's C'Wood Sportin Good, bred with Dr. Patricia Haines. Owned by D. Hardy and Nicholas Urbanek, he won multiple BIS and countless Group placements. There is no doubt that Sally will continue to hit home runs for the Pointer in the show ring.

The Solivia kennel of Susan Olivia Lewis Thompson began in the early 1970s with Irish Setters and English Cockers, but eventually got into Pointers, Susan's childhood pet. Since its inception, Solivia has bred over 120 American and international champions, in all colors including solids. One of the foundation dogs here is Ch. Orion of Crookrise, bred by the Crookrise kennels in England, who, when bred to descendants of the old Truewithem line, produced many champions, including Am./Can. Ch. Solivia's Blackheart Bravado, himself the sire of 26 champions; Ch. Solivia's Baby Bunting, the dam of 13 champions; Ch. Solivia's Briarpatch Bunny; Am./Int. Ch. Solivia's Maid of Cotton, CGC; and many others. Another great Solivia dog is Am./Braz./Mex./Int. Ch. Onsage Marquetry of Solivia, a top international show dog and sire.

Four-time national specialty winner, Ch. Jason of Kinnike won eight BIS awards during his career, which spanned most of the 1980s. He won his first BIS at 14 months of age and his last specialty from the Veterans Class at 8 years old. The historical wins of Ch. Cumbrian Black Pearl, setting a new BIS record for Pointers with 22 all-breed shows, took place in 1984, when she was the number-one Sporting Dog and number-three all-breeds. On her way to the record, she won 84 Groups.

In 1986 Ch. Marjetta National Acclaim won the prestigious BIS award at Westminster. In all, he won 19 BIS awards and became the breed's top sire with 107 champion offspring. "Deputy," as he was called, left his mark on many winning kennels, including Ablearm, Bee Serious, Tahari, Coralwood, Paladen and others.

While we're talking about top producers, we must acknowledge two top-producing dams, Deputy's mom, Ch. Truewithem A Taste of Triumph, dam of 29 champion get, and the reigning top-producing dam Ch. Sydmar the Heartless Wench (Blair), who produced 31 champions in just 4 litters. Her progeny include five BIS and two specialty winners, and she has herself won many prestigious classes.

Ch. Bee Serious Kinsman, BOB at Westminster in 2000, handled by Peter Green. Judge, Houston Clark.

Den and Elsa Lawler began their Bee Serious Pointers in 1985 with Ch. Marjetta Kountry Music, bred by Glen Boyer and Marjorie Martorella. She produced eight champion progeny. In the early 1990s, the Lawlers had great success with the BIS-winning bitch Ch. Marjetta Reatta of Kintyre, bred by Marjorie Martorella, handled by co-owner Cindy Lane. Then came along "Elliott" in 1996: formally Ch. Albelarm's Bee Serious, bred by Mrs. Alan Robson and Michael Zollo, presented by Peter Green and co-owned with Judy and Frank DePaulo and DeeAnne Malanga. By 1997 Ch. Albelarm's Bee Serious won 22 BIS and 122 Group Ones, not to mention Best of Breed at Westminster from 1996 through 1998. These two top-drawer Pointers became the inspiration and foundation of the Bee Serious Pointers. The next great dogs out of Bee Serious were Ch. Bee Serious Kinsman, who became the top Pointer in 1999 and 2000, and Am./Can. Ch. Bee Serious Lord Jim, JH, the top Pointer for 2002.

Three-time national specialty winner Am./Can. Ch. Luftnase Albelarm Bee's Knees, CD, JH became the country's number-one dog all-breeds in 1989. During her career she won 47 Best in Show awards and 147 Group Ones. She was sired by Westminster BIS Ch. Marjetta National Acclaim.

The Kinnike kennels of John and Erica Bandes began in 1979 and has produced over 100 champions, including 4 of the breed's 8 Dual Champions and many titled field dogs. The four Kinnike Dual Champions are DC/AFC Kinnike Wythelde, SH, the breed's first bitch Dual Champion; DC Kinnike Blackthorne; DC/AFC Kinnike Hedda, JH; and DC Kinnike Simon, JH. The Kinnike bloodlines are based on the famous Crookline dogs from England and can be found in the Luftnase and Albelarm stock as well. Among the top dogs here are multi-BIS-winning Ch. Jason of Kinnike, Ch. Kinnike Hannah, CD, JH and Ch. Kinnike Mathilda, JH; both bitches are the dams of two Dual Champions. The next Dual Champion from this kennel should be Ch. Kinnike Stewart JH, totaling five.

Thanks to the dedicated breeders that we've mentioned, many new dogs and kennels continue to enter the show world and finish on top. One such dog is Cheryl Laduc's multi-BIS-winning Ch Cookieland's Life Of Leisure, co-owned with A. Cantor and A. Walker. The Pointer in the US thrives in the show ring and in the field, often dominating the competition and proving that the breed is as near perfection as a pure-bred dog can be.

POINTER

Some remarkable characteristics of the Pointer are the breed's exceptionally high energy level, directness of purpose and zest for life. However, there are also the more subtle and telling things that make the Pointer the unique breed that it is. Living with the breed reveals both the Pointer's innate intelligence and uncanny ability to work things out.

The average Pointer doesn't "need" people: he accepts them. If it were possible to ask your Pointer if he required some assistance, the answer might well be, "I can manage that by myself very well, thank you." A Pointer might think this is so; however, a Pointer must have direction and discipline. You must never forget that this is a dog carefully bred through history for speed, stamina and intelligence—admirable but lethal qualities if not properly channeled.

The Pointer's striking appearance has, in many cases, been the reason for selecting the breed as a household pet. Unfortunately, too often the needs of the breed are ignored. The owner of a Pointer must respond to this highly intelligent breed's athleticism. If he cannot guarantee his dog at least one hour of daily exercise, then there must be someone in the household who can. Then and only then can the Pointer become the ideal family dog. Otherwise, the potential owner should consider a different, less active breed.

If such care and training can be provided, it is still important not to act hastily. For the Pointer who is destined to be an all-around family and house dog, it is better to choose from a breeder who has selected for characteristics that include an eye to the show ring and companionship rather than from a breeder who is concentrating exclusively on hunting. Hunting dogs may be far too active for the family who doesn't require a sporting companion, though it is necessary to screen show breeders carefully as well.

People are attracted to the Pointer for many reasons: his beauty and deportment are legendary. Other owners wax lyrical about the intelligence and ability of Pointers in the field and even in day-to-day life. Besides these attributes, there is a wide range of beautiful colors and markings from which to choose.

However, all of these characteristics do not constitute reason enough for anyone to purchase a Pointer without the prospective owner's conducting a little self-evaluation as well.

This is not a breed that can be left home alone all day long and then be taken out for a ten-minute walk in the evening. Many generations of selective breeding make the Pointer a dog that must run. The breed, no matter from what lines it may come, show or field, has the innate desire to experience the great outdoors and perform its duties as a hunter of game. A Pointer can be a great companion and close friend for his entire life, but only if the owner is ready to invest the time, patience and exercise outdoors required to bring the breed to its full potential.

Pointer pups are very cute. Their floppy ears, elastic physiques and waggy-tail personalities make them irresistible. Indeed, Pointer puppies are the subject of calendars and greeting cards printed around the world each year. It is important to realize, however, that a Pointer puppy will spend only a very small part of his day sitting and looking cute. The far greater part of the day will be spent investigating, digging, chewing, eating and needing to go outdoors, only to immediately insist that he be let back in. Any prospective owner should also remember that puppies experience just as many of the aches and pains and sniffles as any human child on the way to maturity.

It takes time and planning to fulfill the day-to-day needs of a puppy or grown dog. This says nothing of the time required for the many lessons a Pointer must be taught by his master before he understands what he may and may not do.

Some breeds live simply to please their masters in that they always seem ready, willing and able to respond to commands. The Pointer, however, has to know that you are serious about what you ask him to do, and he may have to think about it as well. What is vital to remember is that your Pointer puppy, or even adult, will depend

The Pointer is a very active dog that requires plenty of outdoor exercise; an hour each day is the absolute minimum.

wholly on you for everything he needs and every lesson he must learn. If you are not ready to accept this responsibility, you are not ready to own a Pointer. It will only result in household damage and drudgery on your part, and what should be a joyful relationship will result in a frustrating situation for both you and your dog.

Failure to understand the amount of time and consideration a well-cared-for dog requires is one of the primary reasons for the number of unwanted canines that lose their lives in animal shelters.

MENTAL AND PHYSICAL

Everything in the Pointer's history contributed to the mental and physical characteristics that have produced both an industrious, efficient hunting dog and a fine household companion. Generations of selection on that basis give us dogs that embody what makes a Pointer a Pointer.

Given proper consideration beforehand, the purchase of a dog can bring many years of companionship and comfort as well as the unconditional love and devotion that no other animal can match.

Before any family brings a dog into their home, they should give very serious consideration to three extremely important questions:

1. *Does the person who will ultimately be responsible for the dog's day-to-day care really want a dog?*

The children in the family may vociferously claim that they desperately want a dog; however, will they be doing more than just playing with the dog once he arrives? Pet care can be an excellent way to teach children responsibility, but it should not be forgotten that, in their enthusiasm to have a puppy, children are likely to promise almost anything. It is what will happen *after* the novelty of owning a new dog has worn off that must be considered.

In many active families the ultimate responsibility for the family dog often falls on one person. This appears to be the case even in the homes where both parents work outside the home. This person may not relish any more duties than he or she already has.

2. *Does the lifestyle and schedule of the household lend itself to the demands of proper dog care?*

There must always be someone available to see to a dog's basic needs: feeding, exercise, training and so on. If you or your family are gone from morning to night or if you travel frequently and are away from home for long periods of time, the dog must still be cared for. A Pointer cannot be left home alone day in and day out. Are you willing and able to adjust your schedule, or are you prepared to pay the costs of frequent boarding and/or dogsitting for your dog while you are gone?

3. *Is this particular breed, the Pointer, suitable for the individual or household?*

Does your household contain children? Pointers are wonderful with well-behaved children and they make delightful playmates, but no dog should be expected to tolerate abuse just because a child doesn't know better. At the same time, an enthusiastic Pointer puppy can knock down and injure a toddler in a playful moment.

The prospective dog owner should also strongly consider the specific peculiarities of his own lifestyle and household. Everyone involved must realize that the new dog will not understand the household routine and must be taught everything you want him to know and do. This takes time and patience, and often the most important lessons for the new dog to learn will take the longest for him to absorb.

Your Pointer puppy should have received lots of human and canine interaction at the breeder's home. This socialization helps to mold him into a friendly, well-adjusted, people-loving companion.

WHY A PURE-BRED?

There is no difference in the love, devotion and companionship that a mixed-breed dog and a pure-bred dog can give his owner. There are, however, some aspects that can best be fulfilled by the pure-bred dog.

What will a mixed-breed puppy look like as an adult? If esthetics are important to you and you have a specific image in mind of what your dream dog looks like, you are best off not taking the chance with a mix. For instance, the haystack look

THE DEVOTED "NANNY"

One of the Pointer's most striking characteristics is the kind and gentle manner with which he conducts himself in the company of children. Even the most accomplished field dog has a very special place reserved for youngsters. Many owners state that the speed demon at work in the field can become quite the devoted "nanny" in dealing with the family's children. The Pointer raised with children is as much their protector as their playmate.

not be at all what the owner had hoped for. Then what happens to the dog?

In buying a well-bred Pointer puppy, the purchaser will have a very good idea of what the dog will look like at maturity as well as how he will be capable of behaving with proper guidance. If your mental picture of the ideal dog is a Cocker Spaniel or an English Setter that lives only to lavish attention and affection upon you, the more independent breeds (of which the Pointer is certainly one) are not going to live up to that ideal. Naturally there are differences within breeds just as there are differences from family to family and from human to human. At the same time, the general character of a specific breed is far more predictable than that of a dog of unknown parentage.

When choosing a puppy, one must have the adult dog in mind because the little fellow is going to be an adult much longer than he ever was a puppy. The adult dog is what must fit the owner's lifestyle and esthetic standards. A fastidious housekeeper may well have second thoughts when trying to accommodate a very large breed that slobbers or one that sheds his coat all year 'round. All dogs shed to some degree. Pointer hair is shorter and less noticeable on clothing and furniture but far more difficult than long hair to pick up with a vaccuum cleaner or a brush.

of the Old English Sheepdog would not be suitable for someone who thinks the razor-sharp lines of the Doberman are what the perfect dog should have. Predicting what a mixed-breed puppy will look like at maturity is nearly impossible. Size, length of hair and temperament can change drastically between puppyhood and adulthood and may

EXTRAORDINARY BRAIN POWER

As far back as the 19th century, dog experts attested to the extraordinary brain power of the Pointer. In 1880 Edward Jesse, Esq., noted dog authority and author of *Dog Anecdotes,* wrote, "Thus a pointer has been known to refuse to hunt for a person who had previously missed every bird the dog had found. He left him with every mark of disgust, nor could any coaxing induce him to continue with his unsportsmanlike companion."

The initial purchase price of a Pointer could easily be a significant investment for the owner, but a pure-bred dog costs no more to maintain than a mixed breed, unless of course it is blessed with the coat of a Maltese or Poodle, which the Pointer is not. If the cost of having exactly the kind of dog you want and are proud to own is amortized over the number of years you will enjoy him, you must admit the initial cost becomes far less consequential.

WHO SHOULD OWN A POINTER?

Just as a prospective buyer should have a checklist to lead him to a responsible breeder, so must good breeders have a list of qualifications for the buyer. These are just a few of the "musts" a prospective Pointer buyer might face if looking to purchase a puppy from a responsible breeder:

1. The buyer must have a fenced yard and a secure and protected place for the dog to stay if he is out of the house.
2. Children should be at least five years of age. Although Pointers seem to have a natural affinity for children, an adolescent Pointer can be clumsy and can unintentionally injure a toddler.
3. Pointers are usually too strong and active for elderly people.
4. Everyone in the family must want a Pointer.
5. The buyer must be financially able to provide proper veterinary and home care.
6. No Pointer is likely to be sold to a person who is interested in breeding "just pets" or operating an indiscriminate "stud factory."
7. The buyer must be aware that Pointers require a great deal of exercise.

Pointers are playful dogs who make fun companions. Here's a surfing pup "riding the waves" with a little help from his family.

THE POINTER AS A HOUSE DOG

A young Pointer must start understanding household rules from the moment he enters your home. What it will take to accomplish this is patience, love and a firm but gentle and unrelenting hand. Even the youngest Pointer puppy understands the difference between being corrected and being abused.

Pointers are entirely capable of being anyone's best friend and household companion but, as is the case in any good relationship, both parties must be compatible. Pointers were bred to hunt. At no time in the breed's developmental history was any attempt made to make the Pointer a lap dog or boudoir companion. A Pointer best belongs to someone who realizes that work can come in the form of almost any structured activity—performing the daily obedience routine or even playing ball.

Pointers must be given their daily duties and plenty of opportunity to exercise, or they may well use up their excess time by inventing things to do. What your Pointer decides to do on his own might be gnawing the legs of your best table, digging a tunnel to the neighbor's yard or communicating vocally with every other canine in the hemisphere. As far as your Pointer is concerned, if you do not insist that something he is doing must be stopped, your lack of determination will be construed as *carte blanche* or permission to continue! Pointers learn quickly, but that does not mean they always care about what you are trying to impress upon them. Moreover, if you do not provide the requisite leadership, your Pointer will let you know in no uncertain terms that he is entirely capable of providing that leadership for himself.

The Pointer is short of coat and long on endurance, particularly tolerant of heat and, considering the breed's thin single coat, fairly tolerant of the cold as well. However, the Pointer must still be left in the shade when temperatures soar or housed indoors when they plummet.

The Pointer is curious and will want to roam if not provided with a fenced yard, so a fenced yard or other securely enclosed area is necessary for off-leash exercise and training. The Pointer can be trained to do just about anything a dog is capable of doing, particularly if the task includes agility and enthusiasm.

POINTERS IN THE FIELD
For the individual desiring a hunting partner, the Pointer offers many superb qualities, not the least of which is his short coat that requires little deburring. If you plan to hunt in the uplands over game birds, such as quail, pheasant and grouse, then shooting over a Pointer is the way to go. Hunting with a Pointer is an all-day affair, and this breed knows how to last the entire day, expending his energy like a professional athlete. If you are interested in hunting with your dog in the field but have never done so, attend a walking field trial and observe how the dogs work. The assistance of a professional trainer is invaluable to the novice hunter, equally for the puppy and the owner. The first year in a hunting puppy's life is the most critical time in establishing what kind of hunter the dog will become.

MALE OR FEMALE?
While some people may have personal preferences as to the sex of their dog, both the male and the female Pointer make equally good companions and are equal in their trainability. The decision will have more to do with the lifestyle and ultimate plans of the owner than

with differences between the sexes in the breed.

Pointers from lines bred strictly for the field are usually smaller and finer-boned. They also seem to pack more energy ounce for ounce in their physiques. Pointers from show lines are generally larger and have heavier bone than their field cousins. The male is normally larger and heavier-boned than the female at maturity.

Males usually take a longer time to grow up both mentally and physically. Some males can

In the field, the Pointer is the paragon of hunting prowess, though not the first choice of hunting novices.

reach a point during adolescence when they could not care less about food, and keeping the young male at a reasonable weight may prove to be somewhat of a challenge. This is not to say that young Pointer females are exempt from these disturbing hunger strikes, but

ONE STEP AHEAD

An excellent example of the Pointer's speed and endurance comes from the field. It is said that the reason the Pointer is so successful in the field is that he covers so much ground in the course of a hunt. Many estimate that covering 100 miles in a full day's hunt is not unusual for a big-running Pointer. This, combined with the breed's often unbridled enthusiasm for its work, can result in the dog's becoming quite out of control. None of these characteristics disappears because a Pointer has been chosen as a house dog and companion. Therefore, the owner of a companion Pointer must always be one step ahead of his dog and always in control.

experience has proven that males are apt to take the lead here.

The female is not entirely problem-free. She will have her semi-annual, and sometimes burdensome, heat cycles after she is eight or nine months old. At these times she must be confined so that she will not soil her surroundings, and she must also be closely watched to prevent male dogs from gaining access to her or she will become pregnant.

ALTERING
Spaying the female or neutering the male will not change the personality of your pet and will avoid many problems. Neutering the male Pointer can reduce, if not entirely eliminate, his desire to pursue a neighborhood female that shows signs of an impending romantic attitude.

Neutering or spaying also precludes the possibility of your Pointer's adding to the pet overpopulation problem that concerns animal activists and environmentalists worldwide. Altering also reduces the risk of problems including mammary cancer in the female and testicular and prostate cancer in the male.

HEALTH CONCERNS
With a little luck and grace, the well-cared-for Pointer often lives to be 12 to 14 years of age, acting hale and hearty for most of those years. Unfortunately, all breeds of

HIGH-ENERGY DOG

Pointers are not the best choices as companions for those who live in an apartment. Pointers don't pretend to be city slickers. Hundreds of years have been invested in making the Pointer a wide-ranging, highly energetic dog, and confining the Pointer to close quarters for long periods of time is likely to produce a neurotic, destructive and unhappy dog.

domesticated dog suffer from some hereditary problems, though the Pointer's problems are relatively few.

A chief concern among Pointer breeders is hip dysplasia, commonly referred to as HD. This is a developmental disease of the hip joint. One or both hip joints of the affected dog have abnormal contours. Some dogs might show tenderness in the hip, walk with a limp or swaying gait or experience difficulty getting up. Symptoms vary from mild temporary lameness to severe crippling in extreme cases. Treatment may require surgery. Even though hip dysplasia is not very common in the Pointer, enough cases have been reported to merit breeders' having appropriate testing done on their stock. Owners should ask to see hip clearances on the litter's parents.

Some occasions of a relatively rare and unusual disease known as neurotropic osteopathy have been documented in the breed as well.

What appear to be skeletal injuries occur somewhere in the age range of three to nine months as a result of degeneration of the spinal cord.

There are reports of some skin problems, including demodectic mange. Regular grooming procedures are important in that they prevent any of these skin problems from progressing to an advanced stage.

Eye problems such as entropion and progressive retinal atrophy (PRA) have been recorded by careful breeders, but not on an alarming basis. Here again, purchasing a Pointer from a respected breeder who has eye testing done is extremely important.

Pointers make great cycling companions, if trained to run safely beside the bike.

The Pointer of the proper shape, balance and proportion creates a picture of a lithe, elegant dog of noble carriage, able to perform in the field with speed and agility for the whole day long if necessary. The question that arises, however, is, what tells us if a Pointer does, in fact, have the right make and shape, balance and proportion?

The answers are found in the breed standard. Breed standards are very accurate descriptions of the ideal specimen of a given breed. Standards describe the dog physically, listing all of a breed's anatomical parts and indicating how those parts should look. The standard also describes the breed's temperament and how it should move (gait).

The standard is the blueprint that breeders use to fashion their breeding programs. The goal, of course, is to move one step closer to that ever-elusive picture of perfection with each succeeding generation. A breed standard is also what dog-show judges use to measure which of the dogs being shown compares most favorably to what is required of that breed.

It should be understood that what the standard describes is the perfect dog of a given breed. In nature, nothing is absolutely perfect. Thus the breeder and the judge are looking for the dog that, in their opinion, comes closest to that image of perfection. How each individual person interprets this standard will vary somewhat, and no dog will possess every desired characteristic.

Although it takes many years to fully understand the implications of a breed standard, owners of Pointers should familiarize themselves with the stated requirements of the breed. This will enable the person who wishes to own a Pointer to have a good idea of what a representative specimen should look and act like. Here we present the two important standards for the breed, one adopted by the American Kennel Club and the other by the United Kennel Club, which calls the breed English Pointer.

THE AMERICAN KENNEL CLUB BREED STANDARD FOR THE POINTER

General Appearance
The Pointer is bred primarily for sport afield; he should unmistakably look and act the part. The ideal specimen gives the immediate

impression of compact power and agile grace; the head noble, proudly carried; the expression intelligent and alert; the muscular body bespeaking both staying power and dash. Here is an animal whose every movement shows him to be a wide-awake, hard-driving hunting dog possessing stamina, courage and the desire to go. And in his expression are the loyalty and devotion of a true friend of man.

Temperament
The Pointer's even temperament and alert good sense make him a congenial companion both in the field and in the home. He should be dignified and should never show timidity toward man or dog.

Head
The skull of medium width, approx-imately as wide as the length of the muzzle, resulting in an impression of length rather than width. Slight furrow between the eyes, cheeks cleanly chiseled. There should be a pronounced stop. From this point forward the muzzle is of good length, with the nasal bone so formed that the nose is slightly higher at the tip than the muzzle at the stop. Parallel planes of the skull and muzzle are equally acceptable. The muzzle should be deep without pendulous flews. Jaws ending square and level, should bite evenly or as scissors. Nostrils well developed and wide open. *Ears*—Set on at eye level. When hanging

A modern champion, Ch. Kinnike Mickey of True Colors.

naturally, they should reach just below the lower jaw, close to the head, with little or no folding. They should be somewhat pointed at the tip (never round) and soft and thin in leather. *Eyes*—Of ample size, rounded and intense. The eye color should be dark in contrast with the color of the markings, the darker the better.

Neck
Long, dry, muscular and slightly arched, springing cleanly from the shoulders.

Shoulders
Long, thin and sloping. The top of blades close together.

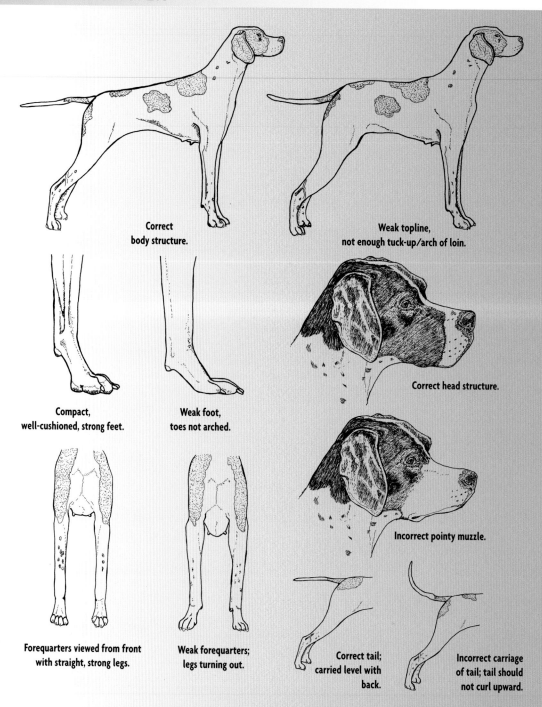

Correct
body structure.

Weak topline,
not enough tuck-up/arch of loin.

Compact,
well-cushioned, strong feet.

Weak foot,
toes not arched.

Correct head structure.

Incorrect pointy muzzle.

Forequarters viewed from front
with straight, strong legs.

Weak forequarters;
legs turning out.

Correct tail;
carried level with
back.

Incorrect carriage
of tail; tail should
not curl upward.

Front

Elbows well let down, directly under the withers and truly parallel so as to work just clear of the body. Forelegs straight and with oval bone. Knee joint never to knuckle over. Pasterns of moderate length, perceptibly finer in bone than the leg and slightly slanting. *Chest*, deep rather than wide, must not hinder free action of forelegs. The breastbone bold, without being unduly prominent. The ribs well sprung, descending as low as the elbow-point.

Back

Strong and solid with only a slight rise from croup to top of shoulders. Loin of moderate length, powerful and slightly arched. Croup falling only slightly to base of tail. Tuck-up should be apparent, but not exaggerated.

Tail

Heavier at the root, tapering to a fine point. Length no greater than to hock. A tail longer than this or docked must be penalized. Carried without curl, and not more than 20 degrees above the line of the back; never carried between the legs.

Hindquarters

Muscular and powerful with great propelling leverage. Thighs long and well developed. Stifles well bent. The hocks clean; the legs straight as viewed from behind.

Decided angulation is the mark of power and endurance.

Feet

Oval, with long, closely-set, arched toes, well-padded, and deep. Catfoot is a fault. Dewclaws on the forelegs may be removed.

Coat

Short, dense, smooth with a sheen.

Color

Liver, lemon, black, orange; either in combination with white or solid-colored. A good Pointer cannot be a bad color. In the darker colors, the nose should be black or brown; in the lighter shades it may be lighter or flesh-colored.

Gait

Smooth, frictionless, with a powerful hindquarters' drive. The head should be carried high, the nostrils wide, the tail moving from side to side rhythmically with the pace, giving the impression of a

Ch. Kinnike Justin is in top condition, showing the typical Pointer pose. Notice the dog's overall musculature, especially evident in the chest and legs.

Lemon-and-white
and black-and-
white are two of
the usual color
combinations seen
in Pointers.

Lemon-and-white and black-and-white are two of the usual color combinations seen in Pointers.

well-balanced, strongly-built hunting dog capable of top speed combined with great stamina. Hackney gait must be faulted.

Balance and Size
Balance and overall symmetry are more important in the Pointer than size. A smooth, balanced dog is to be more desired than a dog with strongly contrasting good points and faults. Hound or terrier characteristics are most undesirable. Because a sporting dog must have both endurance and power, great variations in size are undesirable, the desirable height and weight being within the following limits:

Dogs: *Height*—25–28 inches, *Weight*—55–75 pounds. **Bitches:** *Height*—23–26 inches, *Weight*— 44–65 pounds.

Approved November 11, 1975

THE UNITED KENNEL CLUB STANDARD FOR THE ENGLISH POINTER
History: The Pointer's history is an old one, traceable in writing and in works of art back to the middle of the 17th century. While the

English Pointer was developed primarily in England, most canine historians credit Spain as the country of origin. The English Pointer resulted from crosses between these Spanish pointers and various breeds, most probably Foxhounds and Bloodhounds for scenting, Greyhounds for speed and Bull Terriers for tenacity. Even before the advent of wing shooting with guns, the English Pointer was used to point game, which the hunters then netted or chased with coursing hounds. Pointer breed type, temperament and hunting ability stabilized around the end of the 18th century and have changed very little since then. Today the English Pointer is widely regarded as one of the finest upland bird dogs in the world. The English Pointer was recognized by United Kennel Club in the early 1900s.

General Appearance: The English Pointer is a medium-sized, well-balanced dog with a long, chiseled head; a distinctive "dish" face; small drop ears; and a short, tapered "bee sting" tail carried no higher than 20 degrees above the topline. The length of body is roughly equal to the height at the withers. The distance from the withers to the elbow is roughly equal to the distance from the elbow to the ground. The overall picture is that of an elegant, hard-driving,

intelligent hunter, with stamina and dash. The English Pointer should be evaluated as a working gun dog, and exaggerations or faults should be penalized in proportion to how much they interfere with the dog's ability to work.

Characteristics: The four most distinctive features of the English Pointer are its long, chiseled head, the short "bee sting" tail, strong hunting instincts and effortless, hard-driving movement. The Pointer can be somewhat aloof with strangers but is an excellent family companion, eager to please and particularly good with children.

Head: The head of the English Pointer is the hallmark of this breed. Although the classic "dish face" has become a staple of dog art, the features of the head are as functional as they are beautiful. Viewed from the side, the length of skull and muzzle are approximately equal in length, and joined by a pronounced stop. The topline of the muzzle may be higher at the nose than at the stop or it may be parallel to the topline of the skull. All other things being equal, the dish face is slightly preferred. There is a slight median furrow between the eyes at the forehead and the occipital bone is not conspicuous. Serious fault: Downface.

The skull is long and about half as wide as it is long. The cheeks are flat and well chiseled. Fault: Overly broad skull.

The muzzle must be sufficiently long to allow the dog to carry birds as large as pheasants and grouse. In profile, the muzzle is rectangular. The bridge of the muzzle may rise slightly from stop to nose or be level. Viewed from above, the muzzle is moderately wide with very little taper from stop to nose. Lips are slightly pendant but not overly thick, with pigment to match the nose. The top lip should fall naturally over the lower without folds or drooping, giving a squared appearance to the muzzle when viewed from the side. Fault: Short muzzle.

The English Pointer has a complete set of evenly spaced, white teeth meeting in a scissors or level bite. Faults: Crooked teeth; overshot or undershot bite.

The nose leather may be black or self-colored, depending on coat color. Nostrils must be large and open. Serious fault: Small or restricted nostrils.

The eyes are oval with tight eyelids and pigment to match the nose color. Dogs with black pigment have dark eyes, the darker the better. Lighter-colored eyes are acceptable in dogs with self-colored pigment, but liver-colored dogs should preferably have darker eyes than lemon-colored dogs. The bony arches over the eyes are defined but should not be so excessive as to make the skull appear coarse. Expression is alert and intelligent. Faults: Slanted eyes; sagging eyelids making haw visible.

The English Pointer's ear is another distinguishing mark of the breed. The ears are drop, short in length (reaching just below the lower jaw when hanging naturally) and set on just above eye level. They should be slightly pointed. The ear leather is thin enough that the veins in the ear are apparent. The outer side of the ear is covered with short, silky hair. At rest, the ears should hang nearly flat and close to the cheeks, with little or no fold. Faults: Long, low or rounded ears; thick ear leather.

Neck: The neck is long, slightly arched and muscular. The circumference of the neck widens from the nape to where the neck blends smoothly into well-laid-back shoulders. The skin is tight.

Forequarters: The shoulders are smoothly muscled. The shoulder blades are long and well laid back. The upper arm is roughly equal in length to the shoulder blade and joins it at an apparent right angle. The elbows are close to the body. The forelegs are straight, strong and sturdy, with bone that is oval in shape and proportionate to the overall substance of the dog. Pasterns are

Even at nine years of age, Ch. Kinnike Hannah, CD, JH continues in her winning ways. She is a multiple BIS winner.

BEST OF BREED

OX RIDGE KENNEL CLUB

SEPT. 19, 1992

slightly finer in bone but strong, short and slightly sloping. Faults: Straight shoulders; short upper arm; heavy, round bone; fine bone.

Body: A properly proportioned English Pointer is roughly square in shape. The length of the front legs (measured from point of elbow to the ground) is slightly longer than the deepest part of the body.

The topline is mostly level, never exaggerated or overly sloped, with only a slight rise from the croup to the withers. The back is short, strong and straight. The loin is strong, of moderate length and slightly arched. The croup is slightly sloping. The ribs extend well back and are well sprung out from the spine, then curving down and inward. The forechest extends in a shallow oval shape in front of the forelegs. The chest is deep, reaching to the elbows and of moderate width. Tuck-up is apparent but not exaggerated. Faults: Steeply sloping topline; croup too flat or too steep; tuck-up too exaggerated or absence of tuck-up; excessive skin or "skirting" in the tuck-up; short rib cage with long loin.

Hindquarters: The hindquarters are strong and well muscled. The angulation of the hindquarters is in balance with the angulation of the forequarters. The stifles are well bent, and the hocks are well let down. When the dog is standing, the short, strong rear pasterns are perpendicular to the ground and, viewed from the rear, parallel to one another. Faults: Tilted pelvis resulting in tucked-under hindquarters; straight stifles; thin or poorly-developed second thigh.

The Pointer's dish face is one of the breed's hallmarks. The stop should be pronounced, and the muzzle rises slightly to the tip of the nose.

Feet: Good feet are essential for a working gun dog. Feet are compact, well knit and oval in shape. Toes are long and well arched. Pads are thick and hard. Nails are strong. Front dewclaws may be removed. Faults: Large, round feet; exaggerated hare feet; splayed feet.

Tail: A correct tail is an essential element of English Pointer breed type. The tail is short, reaching no longer than the top of the hock and preferably somewhat shorter. The tail is straight, thicker at the base and tapering to a point. The tail is set on as a natural extension of the topline and should not be carried more than 20 degrees above the topline. When the dog is trotting, the tail moves rhythmically from side to side. Faults: Fat, non-tapering tail; tail carried with curl over the back; long tail. Disqualification: Docked tail.

Coat: The coat is short, dense, close fitting, with a sheen. Faults: Coat too thick and coarse or too thin and sleek; feathering; brushy tail.

Color: Any of the following three coat colors, solid or in combination with white: black, liver and any shade of yellow. Tri-color is also acceptable but is a hound trait and should be faulted accordingly. Dogs with yellow or yellow and white coats that have black noses and eye rims are traditionally referred to as "orange colored." Yellow or yellow and white dogs with liver noses and eye rims are referred to as "lemon colored."

Height and Weight: Desirable height at maturity for males is 25–27 inches and for females, 23–25 inches. Desirable weight for a male in working condition is between 55 and 75 pounds, and between 44 and 65 pounds for a female. Balance and symmetry are more important than size, but great variations in size are undesirable.

Gait: When trotting, the gait is effortless, smooth, powerful and well coordinated, showing good but not exaggerated reach in front and powerful drive behind. The head is carried high and the tail moves from side to side in rhythm with the dog's gait. The backline remains level with only a slight flexing to indicate suppleness. Viewed from any position, legs turn neither in nor out, nor do feet cross or interfere with each other. As speed increases, feet tend to converge toward center line of balance. Poor movement should be penalized to the degree to which it reduces the English Pointer's ability to perform the tasks it was bred to do. Serious fault: Hackney gait.

Disqualifications: Unilateral or bilateral cryptorchid. Viciousness or extreme shyness. Docked tail. Albinism.

Copyright 1992, United Kennel Club, Inc.

POINTER

HOW TO SELECT A POINTER PUPPY

Your Pointer will live with you for many years. Therefore, it is extremely important that the dog comes from a source where physical and mental soundness are primary considerations in the breeding program, usually the result of careful breeding over a period of many years.

Although breeders of Pointers destined primarily for the show ring or as companions take pride in the fact that the dogs they breed have not lost the hunting instinct, other factors are also considered when their breeding stock is selected. Amiability, points of conformation and willingness to keep enthusiasm in check are examples of such desirable characteristics. If you're purchasing a Pointer puppy for purposes of upland game hunting, then the breeder you select will have proven field lines and only breeds dog that have excelled as hunters and trialers.

A good question to ask the breeder of the puppy you are considering is, why does he breed? A responsible breeder will have definite reasons for having produced a litter. The reasons could be varied, because the Pointer is a very adaptable breed, suitable for many purposes. However, if you suspect that the breeder breeds only to sell puppies, it is most advisable that you look elsewhere.

Visiting a breeder's home or kennel gives the buyer the distinct advantage of seeing the parents, or at least the mother, of the puppies that are available. The breeder

Pointers are seen in several colors, and while marking patterns may appear similar and recognizable, each Pointer's markings are unique.

> ### SIGNS OF A HEALTHY PUPPY
> Healthy puppies are robust little fellows who are alert and active, sporting shiny coats and supple skin. They should not appear lethargic, bloated or pot-bellied nor should they have flaky skin or runny or crusted eyes or noses. Their stools should be firm and well formed, with no evidence of blood or mucus.

normally will have other relatives of the dog you are interested in on the premises as well.

Experienced breeders know which hereditary problems exist in the breed and will be willing to discuss them with you. Beware of breeders who tell you that their dogs are not susceptible to inherited diseases or potential problems. We do not mean to imply that all Pointers are afflicted with genetic problems, but a reliable breeder will give you the information you are entitled to know regarding the individual pup you are going to consider.

Inspect the environment in which the dogs are raised. Cleanliness is the first clue that tells you how much the breeder cares about the dogs he owns. Cleanliness is as important to producing good stock as are good pedigrees. The time you spend in researching and inspecting the kennel will save you a great deal

of money and heartache in the years to come.

Above all, the Pointer puppy you buy should be a happy, playful extrovert. Never select a puppy that appears sickly because you feel sorry for him and feel you will be able to nurse him back to good health. Well-bred Pointer puppies with positive temperaments are not afraid of strangers. You should not settle for anything less. Under normal circumstances you will have the whole litter in your lap if you kneel and call them to you.

Check inside the puppy's ears. They should be pink and clean. Any odor or dark discharge could indicate ear mites which, in turn, would indicate poor maintenance. The inside of the puppy's mouth and gums should be pink, and the teeth should be clean and white. There should be no malformation of the mouth or jaw. The eyes

Although some puppies are boisterous and bouncy, others are more laid back.

Housebreaking is
a big part of
puppy training.
Are you ready for
all that dog
ownership
entails?

should be clear and bright. Again, be aware of any signs of discharge. The nose of a Pointer puppy should never be crusted or running.

Pointer puppies should feel compact and substantial to the touch, never bony and undernourished, nor should they be bloated; a taut and bloated abdomen is usually a sign of worms. A rounded puppy belly is normal. Coughing or signs of diarrhea are danger signals as are skin eruptions.

Conformation is important even at an early age. One should remember that the Pointer was originally bred to work in the field the whole day long. Even if the Pointer you buy will never hear a gun or be required to perform as a hunter, the puppy's movement should still be free from impedi-

ment. Limping or stumbling could easily mean lifelong problems.

If you have been reading and doing your research, you can expect the Pointer puppy to look somewhat like a miniaturized version of an adult. Of course, the puppy will not have the elegance and muscularity of a mature dog, but all of the essentials will be there. The puppy's feet may appear too big for the rest of his anatomy, and the ears may seem bigger than they need be, but these are things the youngster will grow into as time passes.

The purchase of any dog is an important step, since the well-cared-for dog will live with you for many years. In the case of a Pointer, this could easily be 12 years or more, years both of you will want to enjoy. Therefore, it is extremely important that your Pointer is purchased from a breeder who has earned a reputa-

TEMPERAMENT ABOVE ALL ELSE

Regardless of breed, a puppy's disposition is perhaps his most important quality. It is, after all, what makes a puppy lovable and "livable." If the puppy's parents or grandparents are known to be snappy or aggressive, the puppy is likely to inherit those tendencies. That can lead to serious problems, such as the dog's becoming a biter, which can lead to eventual abandonment.

tion over the years for consistently producing dogs that are mentally and physically sound.

Unfortunately, the buyer must beware. There are always those who are ready and willing to exploit a breed for financial gain with no thought given to its health or welfare, or to the homes in which the dogs will be living. The Pointer is a very popular breed in the US, no matter what its AKC rank suggests. There are thousands of Pointer fans in every corner of the nation. Look for breeders who belong to a breed club and are active in some area of the dog sport with their Pointers, and get plenty of references.

The only way a breeder can earn a reputation for producing quality animals is through a well-thought-out breeding program in which rigid selectivity is imposed. Selective breeding aims at maintaining the virtues of a breed and eliminating genetic weaknesses. This process is time-consuming and costly. Therefore, responsible Pointer breeders protect their investment by providing the utmost in prenatal care for their dams and maximum care and nutrition for the resulting offspring. Once the puppies arrive, the knowledgeable breeder initiates a proper socialization process.

It is extremely important that the buyer knows the character and quality of a puppy's parents. Good temperament and good health are inherited, and if the puppy's parents are not sound in these respects, there is not much likelihood that they will produce offspring that are. Never

Selecting a Pointer puppy starts with selecting a breeder and observing the litter.

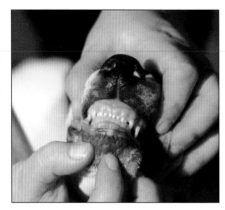

A Pointer puppy showing correct bite. A Pointer should have a scissors bite, meaning that the upper teeth closely overlap the lower teeth.

buy a Pointer from anyone who has no first-hand knowledge of the puppy's parents or what kind of care a puppy has received since birth.

REGISTERING YOUR POINTER PUPPY

The United Kennel Club (UKC) and the American Kennel Club (AKC) are the country's two largest all-breed registries. The UKC refers to our breed as the English Pointer, for purposes of clarity of the breed's origin; the AKC refers to the breed simply as the Pointer, the name used by the English Kennel Club as well. Selecting a registry depends on what the new owner's intentions with his Pointer are. If he wishes to show the dog in an AKC dog show, then purchasing the dog from AKC-registered parents is essential. If the owner wishes to participate in field trials held by the American Field or hunting tests held by the National Shoot to

Retrieve Association (NSTRA), then he must abide by the rules of that organization. Investigating the various registries and clubs online will yield valuable information.

The American Field is the country's oldest registry, established in 1874. It registers kennel names, records field trial wins and publishes a newsletter that includes current registrations. Their Field Dog Stud Book provides registration certificates as well as certified pedigrees to all dogs registered. They are based in Chicago and can be contacted online at www.americanfield.com.

The NSTRA serves as a registry as well as the sponsor of field trials for all pointing dogs, promoting fairness between all pointing breeds and excellent trial quality. Membership inquiries and puppy registrations can be done online at www.nstra.org. The organization is located in Plainfield, Indiana.

The North American Versatile Hunting Dog Association (NAVHDA) is organized to serve the needs of hunters in North America, fostering and improving hunting breeds in the US and promoting game conservation. NAVHDA's activities and services complement those of other registries and field trial clubs. The organization seeks to assist hunters in training their dogs and to provide sportsmen with standard methods of evaluating versatile hunting dogs. They keep accurate records of all test scores as well. NAVHDA offers four types of hunting tests: natural ability test, aimed at evaluating inherited abilities of young dogs; utility preparatory test, geared

Waterfowl hunters can do no better than the Cadillac of gundogs, the Pointer.

toward gauging a dog's development on his way to the utility test; utility test, aimed at evaluating the excellence of field- and water-trained dogs; and the invitational test, intended only for the most highly trained and skilled versatile hunters to test their ability in advanced gundog work. The organization is based in Arlington Heights, Idaho and can be contacted online at www.navhda.org.

PEDIGREE VS. REGISTRATION CERTIFICATE

Too often new owners are confused between these two important documents. Your puppy's pedigree, essentially a family tree, is a written record of a dog's genealogy of three generations or more. The pedigree will show you the names as well as performance titles of all dogs in your pup's background. Your breeder must provide you with a registration application, with his part properly filled out. You must complete the application and send it to the registry (e.g., UKC or AKC) with the proper fee. Every puppy must come from a litter that has been registered by the breeder, born in the US and from a sire and dam that are also registered with the club.

The seller must provide you with complete records to identify the puppy. The registry usually requires that the seller provide the buyer with the following: breed; sex, color and markings; date of birth; litter number (when available); names and registration numbers of the parents; breeder's name; and date sold or delivered.

SHOW DOG, COMPANION OR HUNTER?

We have discussed the primary characteristics of the happy, healthy puppy who will fit the bill as companion and member of the family. However, if you want to be assured of a dog who will be of real show quality, then the fact that the puppy comes from stock known to produce the necessary qualities becomes a major consideration. Also, the older the puppy is at the time of selection, the more likely you will know how

good a dog you will have at maturity. The most any breeder can say about an eight-week-old Pointer puppy is that he has or does not have show or field potential.

If the excitement and pride of owning a winning show dog or outstanding hunting companion appeals to you, we strongly urge you to find a successful breeder who has a record of having produced dogs who have been successful in these endeavors through the years.

For potential owners of field dogs, the advice from a professional gundog trainer is second to none when it comes to finding the right kind of breeder who consistently produces working dogs. When purchasing a field puppy, visit a few kennels and spend time observing the breeder's dogs working in the field. They should be graceful, lithe and powerful, all virtues of this athletic hunting breed. You can trust that the breeder is producing consistent workers, so it is not essential to buy a puppy from the dogs you are watching in the field, but be sure that they are from the same lines. Ask the breeder for references so you can talk to other owners who shoot over his dogs. A professional gundog trainer can steer you in the right direction so that you can find a reputable field breeder and the puppy you start with has the most advantages possible.

GETTING ACQUAINTED

When visiting a litter, ask the breeder for suggestions on how best to interact with the puppies. If possible, get right into the middle of the pack and sit down with them. Observe which pups climb into your lap and which ones shy away. Toss a toy for them to chase and bring back to you. It's easy to fall in love with the puppy who picks you, but keep your future objectives in mind before you make your final decision.

When selecting a puppy for the field, owners often look for accomplishment in field trials in the litter's background. Even though this isn't a guarantee of ability in the pups, it's a hell of a start. As long as you are purchasing a puppy from a proven line, you can be reasonably sure that the puppy you get will have the desired prey drive and natural ability to work. The pup's genealogy promises that he will have the ability to run swiftly, follow scent and handle the stress of the actual hunt. Additionally, a well-bred puppy will have a stronger desire to please you, an important characteristic of the Pointer breed. Do not purchase a Pointer puppy from unproven parents, no matter how good-looking or well-behaved they appear. Puppies from such parents may lack the ability to cover ground or to heed commands in the field; others may be simply out of control, unbiddable and high-strung.

Growing pups may still compete for their morning kibble!

Once you find a top-drawer litter of field Pointers in your lap, you can relax and purchase the puppy that appeals to you. While some puppies will show more dominance, boldness or energy, making them more suitable for a hard day's work, all of the puppies should have the innate trainability and talent you're searching for. If you are the hunter in your family, leave the kids and the gatherers at home. Don't let your family members color your decision. You don't want to break your little girl's heart when she falls in love with a solid-black Pointer puppy that simply doesn't impress you as "the one" for you. You should feel an instant click with your puppy, and that happy sound is the rapport you will build upon in working, training and enjoying your Pointer.

SUPPORT POINTER RESCUE
A non-profit group known as PointerRescue.Org, Inc. (PRO) coordinates the rescue effort for the breed across North America and beyond. If you are interested in rescuing an abandoned Pointer or even fostering a dog or assisting with transports, be certain to contact this worthy rescue group, based in Bridgeton, New Jersey. Donations are also appreciated.

A COMMITTED NEW OWNER
By now you should understand what makes the Pointer a most unique and special dog, one that you feel will fit nicely into your

Young Pointer puppies are mischievous and will have entirely too much fun making a mess of their bedding materials.

family and lifestyle. If you have researched breeders, you should be able to recognize a knowledgeable and responsible Pointer breeder who cares not only about his pups but also about what kind of owner you will be. If you have completed the final step in your new journey, you have found a litter, or possibly two, of quality Pointer pups.

The decision to live with a Pointer is a serious commitment and not one to be taken lightly. This puppy is a living sentient being who will be dependent on you for basic survival for his entire life. Beyond the basics of survival—food, water, shelter and protection—he needs much, much more. The new pup needs love, nurturing and a proper canine education to mold him into a responsible, well-behaved canine citizen. Your Pointer's health and good manners will need consistent monitoring and regular "tune-ups," so your job as a responsible dog owner will be

ongoing throughout every stage of his life. If you are not prepared to accept these responsibilities and commit to them for at least the next decade, likely longer, then you are not prepared to own a dog of any breed.

Although the responsibilities of owning a dog may at times tax your patience, the joy of living with your Pointer far outweighs the workload, and a well-mannered adult dog is worth your time and effort. Before your very eyes, your new charge will grow up to be your most loyal friend!

YOUR POINTER SHOPPING LIST

Just as expectant parents prepare a nursery for their baby, so should you ready your home for the arrival of your Pointer pup. If you have the necessary puppy

---

CRATE EXPECTATIONS

To make the crate more inviting to your puppy, you can offer his first meal or two inside the crate, always keeping the crate door open so that he does not feel confined. Keep a favorite toy or two in the crate for him to play with while inside. You can also cover the crate at night with a lightweight sheet to make it more den-like and remove the stimuli of household activity. Never put him into his crate as punishment or as you are scolding him, since he will then associate his crate with negative situations and avoid going there.

supplies purchased and in place before he comes home, it will ease the puppy's transition from the warmth and familiarity of his mom and littermates to the brand-new environment of his new home and human family. You will be too busy to stock up and prepare your house after your pup comes home, that's for sure! Imagine how a pup must feel upon being transported to a strange new place. It's up to you to comfort him and to let your little pup know that he is going to be happy with you.

FOOD AND WATER BOWLS

Your puppy will need separate bowls for his food and water. Stainless steel pans are generally preferred over plastic bowls since they sterilize better and pups are less inclined to chew on the

From house-training tool to the pup's "bedroom," the return on a quality crate is well worth what it costs. Pictured are the most popular varieties of crate: fabric mesh (LEFT), fiberglass (TOP) and wire (RIGHT).

metal. Heavy-duty ceramic bowls are popular, but consider how often you will have to pick up those heavy bowls. Buy adult-sized bowls, as your Pointer puppy will grow into them before you know it.

THE DOG CRATE

If you think that crates are tools of punishment and confinement for when a dog has misbehaved, think again. Most breeders and almost all trainers recommend a crate as the preferred house-training aid as well as for all-around puppy training and safety. Because dogs are natural den creatures that prefer cave-like environments, the benefits of crate use are many. The crate provides the puppy with his very own "safe house," a cozy place to sleep, take a break or seek comfort with a favorite toy; a travel aid to house your dog when

ROCK-A-BYE BEDDING

The wide assortment of dog beds today can make your choice quite difficult, as there are many adorable novelty beds in fun styles and prints. It's wise to wait until your puppy has outgrown the chewing stage before providing him with a dog bed, since he might make confetti out of it. Your puppy will be happy with an old towel or blanket in his crate until he is old enough to resist the temptation to chew up his bed. For a dog of any age, a bed with a washable cover is always a wise choice.

can be problematic in hot weather. Some of the newer crates are made of heavy plastic mesh; they are very lightweight and fold up into slim-line suitcases. However, a mesh crate might not be suitable for a pup with manic chewing habits.

Don't bother with a puppy-sized crate. Although your Pointer will be a wee fellow when you bring him home, he will grow up in the blink of an eye and your puppy crate will be useless. Purchase a crate that will accommodate an adult Pointer. He can stand up to 28 inches at the shoulder when fully grown, so an extra-large crate, measuring about 48 inches long by 30 inches wide by 36 inches high, will be necessary.

Pointers can be chewers and teething puppies will chew on anything they can get their teeth into. Supply your pup with a variety of durable chew toys, for his safety and the safety of your belongings.

on the road, at motels or at the vet's office; a training aid to help teach your puppy proper toileting habits; a place of solitude when non-dog people happen to drop by and don't want a lively puppy—or even a well-behaved adult dog—saying hello or begging for attention.

Crates come in several types, although the wire crate and the fiberglass airline-type crate are the most popular. Both are safe and your puppy will adjust to either one, so the choice is up to you. The wire crates offer better visibility for the pup as well as better ventilation. Many of the wire crates easily collapse into suitcase-size carriers. The fiberglass crates, similar to those used by the airlines for animal transport, are sturdier and more den-like. However, the fiberglass crates do not collapse and are less ventilated than a wire crate; this

TEETHING TIME

All puppies chew. It's normal canine behavior. Chewing just plain feels good to a puppy, especially during the three- to five-month teething period when the adult teeth are breaking through the gums. Rather than attempting to eliminate such a strong natural chewing instinct, you will be more successful if you redirect it and teach your puppy what he may or may not chew. Correct inappropriate chewing with a sharp "No!" and offer him a chew toy, praising him when he takes it. Don't become discouraged. Chewing usually decreases after the adult teeth have come in.

BEDDING AND CRATE PADS

Your puppy will enjoy some type of soft bedding in his "room" (the crate), something he can snuggle into to feel cozy and secure. Old towels or blankets are good choices for a young pup, since he may (and probably will) have a toileting accident or two in the crate or decide to chew on the bedding material. Once he is fully trained and out of the early chewing stage, you can replace the puppy bedding with a permanent crate pad if you prefer. Crate pads and other dog beds run the gamut from inexpensive to high-end doggie-designer styles, but don't splurge on the good stuff until you are sure that your puppy is reliable and won't tear it up or make a mess on it.

PUPPY TOYS

Just as infants and older children require objects to stimulate their minds and bodies, puppies need toys to entertain their curious brains, wiggly paws and achy teeth. A fun array of safe doggie toys will help satisfy your puppy's chewing instincts and distract him from gnawing on the leg of your antique chair or your new leather sofa. Most puppy toys are cute and look as if they would be a lot of fun, but not all are necessarily safe or good for your puppy, so use caution when you go puppy-toy shopping.

TOYS 'R SAFE

The vast array of tantalizing puppy toys is staggering. Stroll through any pet shop or pet-supply outlet and you will see that the choices can be overwhelming. However, not all dog toys are safe or sensible. Most very young puppies enjoy soft woolly toys that they can snuggle with and carry around. (You know they have outgrown them when they shred them up!) Avoid toys that have buttons, tabs or other enhancements that can be chewed off and swallowed. Soft toys that squeak are fun, but make sure your puppy does not disembowel the toy and remove (and swallow) the squeaker. Toys that rattle or make noise can excite a puppy, but they present the same danger as the squeaky kind and so require supervision. Hard rubber toys that bounce can also entertain a pup, but make sure that the toy is too big for your pup to swallow.

Like many other dogs, Pointers love to chew. The best "chewcifiers" are nylon and hard rubber bones, that are safe to gnaw on and come in sizes appropriate for all age groups and breeds. Be especially careful of natural bones, which can splinter or develop dangerous sharp edges; pups can easily swallow or choke on those bone splinters. Veterinarians often tell of surgical nightmares involving bits of splintered bone because in addition to the danger of choking, the sharp pieces can damage the intestinal tract.

Similarly, rawhide chews, while a favorite of most dogs and puppies, can be equally dangerous. Pieces of rawhide are easily swallowed after they get soft and gummy from chewing, and dogs have been known to choke on pieces of ingested

The collar should fit snugly, but not tightly, around your Pointer's neck and should have the dog's ID tags securely attached.

rawhide. Rawhide chews should be offered only when you can supervise the puppy.

Soft woolly toys are special puppy favorites. They come in a wide variety of cute shapes and sizes; some look like little stuffed animals. Puppies love to shake them up and toss them about or simply carry them around. Be careful of fuzzy toys that have button eyes or noses that your pup could chew off and swallow, and make sure that he does not disembowel a squeaky toy to remove the squeaker! Braided rope toys are similar in that they are fun to chew and toss around, but they shred easily and the strings are easy to swallow. The strings are not digestible and, if the puppy doesn't pass them in his stool, he could end up at the vet's office. As with rawhides, your puppy should be closely monitored with rope toys.

If you believe that your pup has ingested a piece of one of his toys, check his stools for the next couple of days to see if he passes the item when he defecates. At the same time, also watch for signs of intestinal distress. A call to your veterinarian might be in order to get his advice and to be on the safe side.

An all-time favorite toy for puppies (young and old!) is the empty gallon milk jug. Hard plastic juice containers—46 ounces or more—are also excellent. Such containers make lots of noise when they are batted about, and puppies go crazy with delight as they play with them. However, they don't often last very long, so be sure to remove and replace them when they get chewed up.

A word of caution about homemade toys: be careful with your choices of non-traditional play objects. Never use old shoes or socks, since a puppy cannot distinguish between the old ones on which he's allowed to chew and the new ones in your closet that are strictly off limits. That principle applies to anything that resembles something that you don't want your puppy to chew.

COLLARS

A lightweight nylon collar is the best choice for a young pup. Quick-click collars are easy to put on and remove, and they can be adjusted as the puppy grows. Introduce him to his collar as soon as he comes home to get him accustomed to wearing it. He'll get used to it quickly and won't mind a bit. Make sure that it is snug enough that it won't slip off, yet loose enough to be comfortable for the pup. You should be able to slip two fingers between the collar and his neck. Check the collar often, as puppies grow in spurts, and his collar can become too tight almost overnight.

FIRST CAR RIDE

The ride to your home from the breeder will likely be your puppy's first automobile experience, and you should make every effort to keep him comfortable and secure. Bring a large towel or small blanket for the puppy to lie on during the trip and an extra towel in case the pup gets carsick or has a potty accident. It's best to have another person with you to hold the puppy in his lap. Most puppies will fall fast asleep from the rolling motion of the car. If the ride is lengthy, you may have to stop so that the puppy can relieve himself, so be sure to bring a leash and collar for those stops. Avoid rest areas for potty trips, since those are frequented by many dogs, who may carry parasites or disease. It's better to stop at grassy areas near gas stations or shopping centers to prevent unhealthy exposure for your pup.

LEASHES

A 6-foot nylon lead is an excellent choice for a young puppy. It is lightweight and not as tempting to chew as a leather lead. You can switch to a 6-foot leather lead after your pup has grown and is used to walking politely on a lead. For initial puppy walks and house-training purposes, you should invest in a shorter lead so that you have more control over the puppy. At first you don't want him wandering too far away from you,

A Dog-Safe Home

The dog-safety police are taking you on a house tour. Let's go room by room and see how safe your own home is for your new pup. The following items are doggy dangers, so either they must be removed or the dog should be monitored or not allowed access to these areas.

Living Room
- house plants (some varieties are poisonous)
- fireplace or wood-burning stove
- paint on the walls (lead-based paint is toxic)
- lead drapery weights (toxic lead)
- lamps and electrical cords
- carpet cleaners or deodorizers

Outdoors
- swimming pool
- pesticides
- toxic plants
- lawn fertilizers

Bathroom
- blue water in the toilet bowl
- medicine cabinet (filled with potentially deadly bottles)
- soap bars, bleach, drain cleaners, etc.
- tampons

Kitchen
- household cleaners in the kitchen cabinets
- glass jars and canisters
- sharp objects (like kitchen knives, scissors and forks)
- garbage can (with remnants of good-smelling things like onions, potato skins, apple or pear cores, peach pits, coffee beans and other harmful tidbits)
- food left out on counters (some foods are toxic to dogs)

Garage
- antifreeze
- fertilizers (including rose foods)
- pesticides and rodenticides
- pool supplies (chlorine and other chemicals)
- oil and gasoline in containers
- sharp objects, electrical cords and power tools

GOOD CHEWING

Chew toys run the gamut from rawhide chews to hard sterile bones and everything in between. Rawhides are all-time favorites, but they can cause choking when they become mushy from repeated chewing, causing them to break into small pieces that are easy to swallow. Rawhides are also highly indigestible, so many vets advise limiting rawhide treats. Hard sterile bones are great for plaque prevention as well as chewing satisfaction. Dispose of them when the ends become sharp or splintered.

and when taking him out for toileting you will want to keep him in the specific area chosen for his potty spot.

Once the puppy is heel-trained with a traditional leash, you can consider purchasing a retractable lead. A retractable lead is excellent for walking adult dogs that are already leash-wise. This type of lead allows the dog to roam farther away from you and explore a wider area when out walking, and also retracts when you need to keep him close to you. Buy one suitable for your Pointer's adult weight.

HOME SAFETY FOR YOUR PUPPY

The importance of puppy-proofing cannot be overstated. In addition to making your house comfortable for your Pointer's arrival, you also

must make sure that your house is safe for your puppy before you bring him home. There are countless hazards in the owner's personal living environment that a pup can sniff, chew, swallow or destroy. Many are obvious; others are not. Do a thorough advance house check to remove or rearrange those things that could hurt your puppy, keeping any potentially dangerous items out of areas to which he will have access.

Electrical cords are especially dangerous, since puppies view them as irresistible chew toys.

It's important to provide your Pointer with chew toys, inside and outside, so he doesn't "have fun" with any of your valuables or ingest something that can harm him.

This Pointer pup has found some new friends to snuggle with and keep him warm.

Unplug and remove all exposed cords or fasten them beneath baseboards where the puppy cannot reach them. Veterinarians and firefighters can tell you horror stories about electrical burns and house fires that resulted from puppy-chewed electrical cords. Consider this a most serious precaution for your puppy and the rest of your family.

Scout your home for tiny objects that might be seen at a pup's eye level. Keep medication bottles and cleaning supplies well out of reach, and do the same with waste baskets and other trash containers. It goes without saying that you should not use rodent poison or other toxic chemicals in any puppy area and that you must keep such containers safely locked up. You will be amazed at how many places a curious puppy can discover!

Once your house has cleared inspection, check your yard. A sturdy fence, well embedded into the ground, will give your dog a safe place to play and potty. Pointers are curious and very athletic dogs, so at least a 6-foot-high fence will be required to contain an agile youngster or adult. Check the fence periodically for necessary repairs. If there is a weak link or space to squeeze through, you can be sure a determined Pointer will discover it.

The garage and shed can be hazardous places for a pup, as things like fertilizers, chemicals and tools are usually kept there. It's best to keep these areas off limits to the pup. Antifreeze is especially dangerous to dogs, as

ASK THE VET

Help your vet help you to become a well-informed dog owner. Don't be shy about becoming involved in your puppy's veterinary care by asking questions and gaining as much knowledge as you can. For starters, ask what shots your puppy is getting and what diseases they prevent, and discuss with your vet the safest way to vaccinate. Find out what is involved in your dog's annual wellness visits. If you plan to spay or neuter, discuss the best age at which to have this done. Start out on the right "paw" with your puppy's vet and develop good communication with him, as he will care for your dog's health throughout the dog's entire life.

they find the taste appealing and it takes only a few licks from the driveway to kill a dog, puppy or adult, small breed or large.

VISITING THE VETERINARIAN

A good veterinarian is your Pointer puppy's best health-insurance policy. If you do not already have a vet, ask friends and experienced dog people in your area for recommendations so that you can select a vet before you bring your Pointer puppy home. Also arrange for your puppy's first veterinary examination before-hand, since many vets do not have appointments available immediately, and your puppy should visit the vet within a day or so of coming home.

HYF4720

ARE VACCINATIONS NECESSARY?

Vaccinations are recommended for all puppies by the American Veterinary Medical Association (AVMA). Some vaccines are absolutely necessary, while others depend upon a dog's or puppy's individual exposure to certain diseases or the animal's immune history. Rabies vaccinations are required by law in all 50 states. Some diseases are fatal whereas others are treatable, making the need for vaccinating against the latter questionable. Follow your veterinarian's recommendations to keep your dog fully immunized and protected. You can also review the AVMA directive on vaccinations on their website: www.avma.org.

It's important to make sure your puppy's first visit to the vet is a pleasant and positive one. The vet should take great care to befriend the pup and handle him gently to make their first meeting a positive experience. The vet will give the pup a thorough physical examination and set up a schedule for vaccinations and other necessary wellness visits. Be sure to show your vet any health and inoculation records, which you should have received from your breeder. Your vet is a great source of canine health information, so be sure to ask questions and take notes. Creating

Puppies will investigate—it's just part of being a puppy! Supervise your pup to keep him out of danger, and keep any potentially harmful items out of his reach.

A securely enclosed yard is helpful in providing your Pointer with the free-running time he needs within safe boundaries.

a health journal for your puppy will make a handy reference for his wellness and any future health problems that may arise.

MEETING THE FAMILY

Your Pointer's homecoming is an exciting time for all members of the family, and it's only natural that everyone will be eager to meet him, pet him and play with him. However, for the puppy's sake, it's best to make these initial family meetings as uneventful as possible so that the pup is not overwhelmed with too much too soon. Remember, he has just left his dam and his littermates and is away from the breeder's home for the first time. Despite his ever-wagging tail, he is still apprehensive and wondering where he is and who all these strange humans are. It's best to let him explore on his own and meet the family members as he feels comfortable. Let him investigate all the new smells, sights and sounds at his own pace. Children should be especially careful to not get overly excited, use loud voices or hug the pup too tightly. Be calm, gentle and affectionate, and be ready to comfort him if he appears frightened or uneasy.

Be sure to show your puppy his new crate during this first day home. Toss a treat or two inside the crate; if he associates the crate with food, he will associate the crate with good things. If he is comfortable with the crate, you can offer him his first meal inside it. Leave the door ajar so he can wander in and out as he chooses.

FIRST NIGHT IN HIS NEW HOME

So much has happened in your Pointer puppy's first day away from the breeder. He's had his first

HAPPY PUPPIES COME RUNNING

Never call your puppy (or adult dog) to come to you and then scold him or discipline him when he gets there. He will make a natural association between coming to you and being scolded, and he will think he was a bad dog for coming to you. He will then be reluctant to come whenever he is called. Always praise your puppy every time he comes to you.

car ride to his new home. He's met his new human family and perhaps the other family pets. He has explored his new house and yard, at least those places where he is to be allowed during his first weeks at home. He may have visited his new veterinarian. He has eaten his first meal or two away from his dam and litter-mates. Surely that's enough to tire out an eight-week-old Pointer pup...or so you hope!

It's bedtime. During the day, the pup investigated his crate, which is his new den and sleeping space, so it is not entirely strange to him. Line the crate with a soft towel or blanket that he can snuggle into and gently place him into the crate for the night. Some breeders send home a piece of bedding from where the pup slept with his littermates, and those familiar scents are a great comfort for the puppy on his first night without his siblings.

He will probably whine or cry. The puppy is objecting to the confinement and the fact that he is alone for the first time. This can be a stressful time for you as well as for the pup. It's important that you remain strong and don't let the puppy out of his crate to comfort him. He will fall asleep eventually. If you release him, the puppy will learn that crying means "out" and will continue that habit. You are laying the groundwork for future habits. Some breeders find that soft music can soothe a crying pup and help him get to sleep.

SOCIALIZING YOUR PUPPY

The first 20 weeks of your Pointer puppy's life are the most important. A properly socialized puppy will grow up to be a

The puppy's socialization began at the breeder's with littermates and visitors to the kennel. You must become your puppy's social director once he arrives at your home.

When you bring your Pointer puppy home, everything will be new to him. Give him time to explore and get used to all of the sights, scents and sounds.

confident and stable adult who will be a pleasure to live with and a welcome addition to the neighborhood.

The importance of socialization cannot be overemphasized. Research on canine behavior has proven that puppies who are not exposed to new sights, sounds, people and animals during their first 20 weeks of life will grow up to be timid and fearful, even aggressive, and unable to flourish outside of their familiar home environment.

Socializing your puppy is not difficult and, in fact, will be a fun time for you both. Lead training goes hand in hand with socialization, so your puppy will be learning how to walk on a lead at the same time that he's meeting the neighborhood. Because the Pointer is such an outgoing, fun-loving breed, everyone will enjoy meeting "the new kid on the block." Take him for short walks to the park and to other dog-friendly places where he will encounter new people, especially

children. Puppies automatically recognize children as "little people" and are drawn to play with them. Just make sure that you supervise these meetings and that the children do not get too rough or encourage him to play too vigorously. An overzealous pup can often nip too hard, frightening the child and in turn making the puppy overly excited. A bad experience in puppyhood can impact a dog for life, so a pup that has a negative experience with a child may grow up to be shy or even aggressive around children.

Take your puppy along on your daily errands. Puppies are natural "people magnets," and most people who see your pup will want to pet him. All of these

MEET AND MINGLE

Puppies need to meet people and see the world if they are to grow up confident and unafraid. Take your puppy with you on everyday outings and errands. On-lead walks around the neighborhood and to the park offer the pup good exposure to the goings-on of his new human world. Avoid areas frequented by other dogs until your puppy has had his full round of puppy shots; ask your vet when your pup will be properly protected. Arrange for your puppy to meet new people of all ages every week.

encounters will help to mold him into a confident adult dog. Likewise, you will soon feel like a confident, responsible dog owner, rightly proud of your mannerly Pointer.

Be especially careful of your puppy's encounters and experiences during the eight- to ten-week-old period, which is also called the "fear period." This is a serious imprinting period, and all contact during this time should be gentle and positive. A frightening or negative event could leave a permanent impression that could affect his future behavior if a similar situation arises.

Also make sure that your puppy has received his first and second rounds of vaccinations before you expose him to other dogs or bring him to places that other dogs may frequent. Avoid dog parks and other strange-dog areas until your vet assures you that your puppy is fully immunized and resistant to the diseases that can be passed between canines. Discuss socialization with your breeder, as some breeders recommend socializing the puppy even before he has received all of his inoculations, depending on how outgoing the puppy may be.

LEADER OF THE PUPPY'S PACK

Like other canines, your puppy needs an authority figure, someone he can look up to and regard as the leader of his "pack." His first pack leader was his dam, who taught him to be polite and not chew too hard on her ears or nip at her muzzle. He learned those same lessons from his littermates. If he played too rough, they cried in pain and stopped the game, which sent an important message to the rowdy puppy.

As puppies play together, they are also struggling to determine who will be the boss. Being pack animals, dogs need someone to be in charge. If a litter of puppies remained together beyond puppyhood, one of the pups would emerge as the strongest one, the one who calls the shots.

Once your puppy leaves the pack, he will look intuitively for a

Raised together since puppyhood, this Pointer and his Boston Terrier housemate are the best of friends.

Set the house rules from the outset. If you don't want to give up a spot on the couch to your Pointer, the time to let him know is in puppyhood.

new leader. If he does not recognize you as that leader, he will try to assume that position for himself. Of course, it is hard to imagine your adorable Pointer puppy trying to be in charge when he is so small and seemingly helpless. You must remember that these are natural canine instincts. Do not cave in and allow your pup to get the upper "paw"!

Just as socialization is so important during these first 20 weeks, so too is your puppy's early education. He was born without any bad habits. He does not know what is good or bad behavior. If he does things like nipping and digging, it's because he is having fun and doesn't know that humans consider these things as "bad." It's your job to teach him proper puppy manners, and this is the best time to accomplish that—before he has developed bad habits, since it is much more difficult to "unlearn" or correct unacceptable learned behavior

than to teach good behavior from the start.

Make sure that all members of the family understand the importance of being consistent when training the new puppy. If you tell the puppy to stay off the sofa and your daughter allows him to cuddle on the couch to watch her favorite television show, your pup will be confused about what he is and is not allowed to do. Have a family conference before your pup comes home so that everyone understands the basic principles of puppy training and the rules you have set forth for the pup, and agrees to follow them.

The old saying that "an ounce of prevention is worth a pound of cure" is especially true when it comes to puppies. It is much easier to prevent inappropriate behavior than it is to change it. It's also easier and less stressful for the pup, since it will keep

A SMILE'S WORTH A MILE
Don't embark on your puppy's training course when you're not in the mood. Never train your puppy if you're feeling grouchy or impatient with him. Subjecting your puppy to your bad mood is a bad move. Your pup will sense your negative attitude, and neither of you will enjoy the session or have any measure of success. Always begin and end your training sessions on a happy note.

discipline to a minimum and create a more positive learning environment for him. That, in turn, will also be easier on you!

Here are a few commonsense tips to keep your belongings safe and your puppy out of trouble:

- Keep your closet doors closed and your shoes, socks and other apparel off the floor so your puppy can't get to them.
- Keep a secure lid on the trash container or put the trash where your puppy can't dig into it. He can't damage what he can't reach!
- Supervise your puppy at all times to make sure he is not getting into mischief. If he starts to chew the corner of the rug, you can distract him instantly by tossing a toy for him to fetch. You also will be able to whisk him outside when you notice that he is about to piddle on the carpet. If you can't see your puppy, you can't teach him or correct his behavior.

SOLVING PUPPY PROBLEMS

CHEWING AND NIPPING

Nipping at fingers and toes is normal puppy behavior. Chewing is also the way that puppies investigate their surroundings. However, you will have to teach your puppy that chewing anything other than his toys is not acceptable. That won't happen overnight and at times puppy

teeth will test your patience. However, if you allow nipping and chewing to continue, just think about the damage that a mature Pointer can do with a full set of adult teeth.

Whenever your puppy nips your hand or fingers, cry out "Ouch!" in a loud voice, which should startle your puppy and stop him from nipping, even if only for a moment. Immediately distract him by offering a small treat or an appropriate toy for him to chew instead (which means having chew toys and puppy treats handy or in your pockets at all times). Praise him when he takes the toy and tell him what a good fellow he is. Praise is just as or even more important in puppy training as discipline and correction.

Puppies also tend to nip at children more often than adults, since they perceive little ones to be more vulnerable and more

Pointer pups love to have fun, and they certainly enjoy the company of a playful pal.

MAKE A COMMITMENT

Dogs are most assuredly man's best friend, but they are also a lot of work. When you add a puppy to your family, you also are adding to your daily responsibilities for years to come. Dogs need more than just food, water and a place to sleep. They also require training (which can be ongoing throughout the lifetime of the dog), activity to keep them physically and mentally fit and hands-on attention every day, plus grooming and health care. Your life as you now know it may well disappear! Are you prepared for such drastic changes?

similar to their littermates. Teach your children appropriate responses to nipping behavior. If they are unable to handle it themselves, you may have to intervene. Puppy nips can be quite painful, and a child's fright-ened reaction will only encourage a puppy to nip harder, which is a natural canine response. As with all other puppy situations, interaction between your Pointer puppy and children should be supervised.

Chewing on objects, not just family members' fingers and ankles, is also normal canine behavior that can be especially tedious (for the owner, not the pup) during the teething period when the puppy's adult teeth are coming in. At this stage, chewing just plain feels good. Furniture legs and cabinet corners are common puppy favorites. Shoes and other personal items also taste pretty good to a pup.

The best solution is, once again, prevention. If you value something, keep it tucked away and out of reach. You can't hide your dining-room table in a closet, but you can try to deflect the chewing by applying a bitter product made just to deter dogs from chewing. Available in a spray or cream, this substance is vile-tasting, although safe for dogs, and most puppies will avoid the forbidden object after one tiny taste. You also can apply the product to your leather leash if the puppy tries to chew on his lead during leash-training sessions.

Keep a ready supply of safe chews handy to offer your Pointer as a distraction when he starts to chew on something that's a "no-no." Remember, at this tender age he does not yet know what is permitted or forbidden, so you have to be "on call" every minute he's awake and on the prowl.

You may lose a treasure or two during your puppy's growing-up period, and the furniture could sustain a nasty nick or two. These can be trying times, so be prepared for those inevitable accidents and comfort yourself in knowing that this too shall pass.

Puppy Whining

Puppies often cry and whine, just as infants and little children do. It's their way of telling us that they are lonely or in need of attention. Your puppy will miss his littermates and will feel insecure when he is left alone. You may be out of the house or just in another room, but he will still feel alone. During these times, the puppy's crate should be his personal comfort station, a place all his own where he can feel safe and secure. Once he learns that being alone is okay and not something to be feared,

he will settle down without crying or objecting. You might want to leave a radio on while he is crated, as the sound of human voices can be soothing and will give the impression that people are around.

Give your puppy a favorite cuddly toy or chew toy to entertain him whenever he is crated. You will both be happier: the puppy because he is safe in his den and you because he is quiet, safe and not getting into puppy escapades that can wreak havoc in your house or cause him danger.

To make sure that your puppy will always view his crate as a safe and cozy place, never, ever use the crate as punishment. That's the best way to turn the crate into a negative place that the pup will want to avoid. Sure, you can use the crate for your own peace of mind if your puppy is getting into trouble and needs some "time out." Just don't let him know that! Never scold the pup and immediately place him into the crate. Count to ten, give him a couple of hugs and maybe a treat, then scoot him into his crate.

It's also important not to make a big fuss when he is released from the crate. That will make getting out of the crate more appealing than being in the crate, which is just the opposite of what you are trying to achieve.

DIGGING OUT

Some dogs love to dig. Others wouldn't think of it. Digging is considered "self-rewarding behavior" because it's fun! Of all the digging solutions offered by the experts, most are only marginally successful and none are guaranteed to work. The best cure is prevention, which means removing the dog from the offending site when he digs as well as distracting him when you catch him digging so that he turns his attentions elsewhere. That means that you have to supervise your dog's yard time. An unsupervised digger can create havoc with your landscaping or, worse, run away!

Adding a Pointer to your household means adding a new family member who will need your care each and every day. When your Pointer pup first comes home, you will start a routine with him so that, as he grows up, your dog will have a daily schedule just as you do. The aspects of your dog's daily care will likewise become regular parts of your day, so you'll both have a new schedule. Dogs learn by consistency and thrive on routine: regular times for meals, exercise,

A well-fed, happy dog will surely remain man's best friend. Feed your Pointer pal a nutritionally complete dog food in order to maintain good health.

training and potty trips are just as important for your dog as they are for you! Your dog's schedule will depend much on your family's daily routine, but remember that you now have a new member of the family who is part of your day every day.

FEEDING

Feeding your dog the best diet is based on various factors, including age, activity level, overall condition and size of breed. When you visit the breeder, he will share with you his advice about the proper diet for your dog based on his experience with the breed and the foods with which he has had success. Likewise, your vet will be a helpful source of advice throughout the dog's life and will aid you in planning a diet for optimal health.

FEEDING THE PUPPY

Of course, your pup's very first food will be his dam's milk. There may be special situations in which pups fail to nurse, necessitating that the breeder hand-feed them with a formula, but for the most part pups spend the first weeks of life nursing from their dam. The breeder weans the pups by gradually introducing solid foods and decreasing the milk meals. Pups may even start themselves off on the weaning process, albeit inadvertently, if they snatch bites from their mom's food bowl.

By the time the pups are ready for new homes, they are fully weaned and eating a good puppy food. As a new owner, you may be thinking, "Great! The breeder has taken care of the hard part." Not so fast.

A puppy's first year of life is the time when all or most of his

VARIETY IS THE SPICE

Although dog-food manufacturers contend that dogs don't like variety in their diets, studies show quite the opposite to be true. Dogs would much rather vary their meals than eat the same old chow day in and day out. Dry kibble is no more exciting for a dog than the same bowl of bran flakes would be for you. Fortunately, there are dozens of varieties available on the market, and your dog will likely show preference for certain flavors over others. A word of warning: don't overdo it or you'll develop a fussy eater who only prefers chopped beef fillet and asparagus tips every night.

growth and development takes place. This is a delicate time, and diet plays a huge role in proper skeletal and muscular formation. Improper diet and exercise habits can lead to damaging problems that will compromise the dog's health and movement for his entire life. That being said, new owners should not worry needlessly. With the myriad types of food formulated specifically for growing pups of different-sized breeds, dog-food manufacturers have taken much of the guesswork out of feeding your puppy well. Since growth-food formulas are designed to provide the nutrition that a growing puppy needs, it is unnecessary and, in fact, can prove harmful to add supplements to the diet. Research has shown that too much of certain vitamin supplements and minerals predispose a

As your Pointer matures, his dietary needs change as well. Establishing a mealtime routine is vital to properly rearing your pup.

SWITCHING FOODS

There are certain times in a dog's life when it becomes necessary to switch his food; for example, from puppy to adult food and then from adult to senior-dog food. Additionally, you may decide to feed your pup a different type of food from what he received from the breeder, and there may be "emergency" situations in which you can't find your dog's normal brand and have to offer something else temporarily. Anytime a change is made, for whatever reason, the switch must be done gradually. You don't want to upset the dog's stomach or end up with a picky eater who refuses to eat something new. A tried-and-true approach is, over the course of about a week, to mix a little of the new food in with the old, increasing the proportion of new to old as the days progress. At the end of the week, you'll be feeding his regular portions of the new food, and he will barely notice the change.

The breeder will have started your Pointer pup on solid food and can give you advice on what to feed. Any changes in diet should be gradually introduced.

digestive system, his daily portion will be divided up into small meals throughout the day. This can mean starting off with three or more meals a day and decreasing the number of meals as the pup matures. For the adult, dividing the day's food into two meals on a morning/evening schedule, rather than one large daily portion, is recommended for bloat prevention.

Regarding the feeding schedule, feeding the pup at the same times and in the same place each day is important for both housebreaking purposes and establishing the dog's everyday routine. As for the amount to feed, growing puppies generally need proportionately more food per body weight than their adult counterparts, but a pup should

dog to skeletal problems. It's by no means a case of "if a little is good, a lot is better." At every stage of your dog's life, too much or too little in the way of nutrients can be harmful, which is why a manufactured complete food is the easiest way to know that your dog is getting what he needs.

Because of a young pup's small body and accordingly small

never be allowed to gain excess weight. Dogs of all ages should be kept in proper body condition, but extra weight can strain a pup's developing frame, causing skeletal problems.

Watch your pup's weight as he grows and, if the recommended amounts seem to be too much or too little for your pup, consult the vet about appropriate dietary changes. Keep in mind that treats, although small, can quickly add up throughout the day, contributing unnecessary calories. Treats are fine when used prudently; opt for dog treats specially formulated to be healthy or for nutritious snacks like small pieces of cheese or cooked chicken.

FEEDING THE ADULT DOG

For the adult (meaning physically mature) dog, feeding properly is about maintenance, not growth. Again, correct weight is a concern. Your dog should appear fit and should have an evident "waist." His ribs should not be protruding (a sign of being underweight), but they should be covered by only a slight layer of fat. Under normal circumstances, an adult dog can be maintained fairly easily with a high-quality nutritionally complete adult-formula food.

Factor treats into your dog's overall daily caloric intake, and avoid offering table scraps. Some

---

FEEDING ACTIVE DOGS

The more a dog does, the more he needs to eat! Examples of dogs with higher nutrient requirements are dogs who are very active in training for or competing in sporting disciplines, and dogs that are used in a working capacity such as hunting. They do not need supplementation to their regular food; rather, because they need larger amounts of all nutrients, they will need their maintenance food in larger portions. Also ask your vet about specially formulated "performance" diets for active dogs.

When feeding an active dog, it is essential to provide adequate periods of rest before and after eating to avoid stomach upset or the more serious gastric torsion, which can be fatal. Treats can be fed during rest periods as well to keep up the dog's energy in between meals, and plenty of water given. The dog needs time to settle down before and after any eating or drinking, so breaks should be factored into the training program or work routine.

"people food," like chocolate, nuts, grapes, raisins, onions and large quantities of garlic, are toxic to dogs; you also do not want to encourage begging or overeating. Overweight dogs are more prone to health problems. Research has even shown that obesity takes years off a dog's life. With that in mind, resist the urge to overfeed and over-treat. Don't make

If it were up to him, your Pointer would probably eat everything in sight. That means it's up to you to watch your dog's weight, especially as he grows older and exercises less.

as with the puppy, the adult dog should have consistency in his mealtimes and feeding place. In addition to a consistent routine, regular mealtimes also allow the owner to practice essential bloat preventives (see later in chapter) and to see how much his dog is eating. If the dog seems never to be satisfied or, likewise, becomes uninterested in his food, the owner will know right away that something is wrong and can consult the vet.

DIETS FOR THE AGING DOG

A good rule of thumb is that once a dog has reached 75% of his expected lifespan, he has reached "senior citizen" or geriatric status. Your Pointer will be considered a senior at about 8 or 9 years of age; he has a projected lifespan of about 12 to 14 years.

What does aging have to do with your dog's diet? No, he won't get a discount at the local diner's early-bird special. Yes, he will require some dietary changes to accommodate the changes that come along with increased age. One change is that the older dog's dietary needs become more similar to that of a puppy. Specifically, dogs can metabolize more protein as youngsters and seniors than in the adult-maintenance stage. Discuss with your vet whether you need to switch to a higher-protein or senior-formulated food or whether your

unnecessary additions to your dog's diet, whether with tidbits or with extra vitamins and minerals.

The amount of food needed for proper maintenance will vary depending on the individual dog's activity level, but you will be able to tell whether the daily portions are keeping him in good shape. With the wide variety of good complete foods available, choosing what to feed is largely a matter of personal preference. Just

THE DARK SIDE OF CHOCOLATE

From a tiny chip to a giant rabbit, chocolate—in any form—is not your dog's friend. Whether it's an Oreo® cookie, a Snickers® bar or even a couple of M&M's®, you should avoid these items with your dog. You are also well advised to avoid any bone toy that is made out of fake chocolate or any treat made of carob—anything that encourages your dog to become a "chocoholic" can't be helpful. Before you toss your pooch half of your candy bar, consider that as little as a single ounce of chocolate can poison a 30-pound dog. Theobromine, like caffeine, is a methylxanthine and occurs naturally in cocoa beans. Dogs metabolize theobromine very slowly, and its effect on the dog can be serious, harming the heart, kidneys and central nervous system. Dark or semi-sweet chocolate is even worse than milk chocolate, and baking chocolate and cocoa mix are by far the worst.

current adult-dog food contains sufficient nutrition for the senior.

Watching the dog's weight remains essential, even more so in the senior stage. Older dogs are already more vulnerable to illness, and obesity only contributes to their susceptibility to problems. As the older dog becomes less active and thus exercises less, his regular portions may cause him to gain weight. At this point, you may consider decreasing his daily food intake or switching to a reduced-calorie food. As with other changes, you should consult your vet for advice.

TYPES OF FOOD AND READING THE LABEL

When selecting the type of food to feed your dog, it is important to check out the label for ingredients. Many dry-food products have soybean, corn or rice as the main ingredient. The main ingredient will be listed first on the label, with the rest of the ingredients following in descending order according to their proportion in the food. While these types of dry food are fine, you should look into dry foods based on meat or fish. These are better-quality foods and thus higher priced. However, they may be just as economical in the long run, because studies have shown that it takes less of the higher-quality foods to maintain a dog.

Comparing the various types of food, dry, canned and semi-moist, dry foods contain the least amount of water and canned foods the most. Proportionately, dry foods are the most calorie- and nutrient-dense, which means that you need more of a canned food product to supply the same amount of nutrition. In households domiciling breeds of disparate size, the canned/dry/

Your Pointer may love people snacks, but that doesn't mean they love him back. Many human treats contain ingredients that can be harmful to a dog, so be careful not to leave these temptations within his reach.

semi-moist question can be of special importance. Larger breeds obviously eat more than smaller ones and thus in general do better on dry foods, but smaller breeds do fine on canned foods and require "small bite" formulations to protect their small mouths and teeth if fed dry foods. So if you have breeds of different sizes in your household, consider both your own preferences and what your dogs like to eat, but mainly think canned for the little guys and dry or semi-moist for everyone else. You may find success mixing the food types as well. Water is important for all dogs, but even more so for those fed dry foods, as there is no high water content in their food.

There are strict controls that regulate the nutritional content of dog food, and a food has to meet

the minimum requirements in order to be considered "complete and balanced." It is important that you choose such a food for your dog, so check the label to be sure that your chosen food meets the requirements. If not, look for a food that clearly states on the label that it is formulated to be complete and balanced for your dog's particular stage of life.

Recommendations for amounts to feed will also be indicated on the label. You should also ask your vet about proper food portions, and you will keep an eye on your dog's condition to see whether the recommended amounts are adequate. If he becomes over- or underweight, you will need to make adjustments; this also would be a good time to consult your vet.

DIET DON'TS

- Got milk? Don't give it to your dog! Dogs cannot tolerate large quantities of cows' milk, as they do not have the enzymes to digest lactose.
- You may have heard of dog owners who add raw eggs to their dogs' food for a shiny coat or to make the food more palatable, but consumption of raw eggs too often can cause a deficiency of the vitamin biotin.
- Avoid feeding table scraps, as they will upset the balance of the dog's complete food. Additionally, fatty or highly seasoned foods can cause upset canine stomachs.
- Do not offer raw meat to your dog. Raw meat can contain parasites; it also is high in fat.
- Vitamin A toxicity in dogs can be caused by too much raw liver, especially if the dog already gets enough vitamin A in his balanced diet, which should be the case.
- Bones like chicken, pork chop and other soft bones are not suitable, as they easily splinter.

The food label may also make feeding suggestions, such as whether moistening a dry-food product is recommended. Sometimes a splash of water will make the food more palatable for the dog and even enhance the flavor. Don't be overwhelmed by the many factors that go into feeding your dog. Manufacturers of complete and balanced foods make it easy, and once you find the right food and amounts for your Pointer, his daily feeding will be a matter of routine.

DON'T FORGET THE WATER!

Regardless of what type of food your Pointer eats, there's no doubt that he needs plenty of water. Fresh cold water, in a clean bowl, should be available to your dog. There are special circumstances, such as during puppy house-breaking, when you will want to monitor your pup's water intake so that you will be able to predict when he will need to relieve himself, but water must be available to him nonetheless. Water is essential for hydration and proper body function just as it is in humans.

You will get to know how much your dog typically drinks in a day. Of course, in the heat or if exercising vigorously, he will be more thirsty and will drink more.

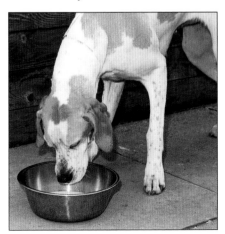

Despite most dogs' affinity for cow's milk, it is not agreeable with their digestive systems. Feeding your Pointer cow's milk is just asking for trouble.

As a safeguard to prevent bloat, do not let your Pointer engage in vigorous activity before or after his meals.

However, if he begins to drink noticeably more water for no apparent reason, this could signal any of various problems, and you are advised to consult your vet.

Water is the best drink for dogs. Some owners are tempted to give milk from time to time or to moisten dry food with milk, but dogs do not have the enzymes necessary to digest the lactose in milk, which is much different

It's always a question of how to exercise: the best answer to the high-energy Pointer is another Pointer to run with.

from the milk that nursing puppies receive. Therefore stick with clean fresh water to quench your dog's thirst.

A word of caution concerning your deep-chested dog's water intake: he should never be allowed to gulp water, especially at mealtimes. In fact, his water intake should be limited at and after mealtimes as a rule. This simple daily precaution can go a long way in protecting your dog from the dangerous and potentially fatal gastric torsion (bloat).

EXERCISE
Food, water and exercise: it is impossible to have a happy, healthy Pointer without sufficient amounts of each. The bored, inactive Pointer would be extremely unhappy and more than capable of wreaking havoc in a confining environment.

The family Pointer can make an ideal jogging companion, an enthusiastic agility and obedience candidate and an excellent field-trial dog. It is the owner's decision. Puppies should never be forced to exercise. Normally, Pointer puppies are little dynamos of energy and keep themselves busy all day long, interspersed with frequent naps. A Pointer should never be subjected to an intense exercise program (like jogging) before he has reached full maturity.

What Is "Bloat" and How Do I Prevent it?

You likely have heard the term "bloat," which refers to gastric torsion (gastric dilatation/volvulus), a potentially fatal condition. It is directly related to feeding and exercise practices, and a brief explanation here is warranted. The term *dilatation* means that the dog's stomach is filled with air, while *volvulus* means that the stomach is twisted around on itself, blocking the entrance/exit points. Dilatation/volvulus is truly a deadly combination, although they also can occur independently of each other. An affected dog cannot digest food or pass gas, and blood cannot flow to the stomach, causing accumulation of toxins and gas along with great pain and rapidly occuring shock.

Many theories exist on what exactly causes bloat, but we do know that deep-chested breeds are more prone. Activities like eating a large meal, gulping water, strenuous exercise too close to mealtimes or a combination of these factors can contribute to bloat, though not every case is directly related to these more well-known causes. With that in mind, we can focus on incorporating simple daily preventives and knowing how to recognize the symptoms. In addition to the tips presented in this book, ask your vet about how to prevent and recognize bloat. An affected dog needs immediate veterinary attention, as death can result quickly. Signs include obvious restlessness/discomfort, crying in pain, drooling/excessive salivation, unproductive attempts to vomit or relieve himself, visibly bloated appearance and collapsing. Do not wait: get to the vet *right away* if you see any of these symptoms. The vet will confirm by x-ray if the stomach is bloated with air; if so, the dog must be treated *immediately*.

As varied as the causes of bloat are the tips for prevention, but some common preventive methods follow:
• Feed two or three small meals daily rather than one large one;
• Do not feed water before, after or with meals, but allow access to water at all other times;
• Never permit rapid eating or gulping of water;
• No exercise for the dog at least two hours before and (especially) after meals;
• Feed high-quality food with adequate protein, adequate fiber content and not too much fat and carbohydrate;
• Explore herbal additives, enzymes or gas-reduction products (only under a vet's advice) to encourage a "friendly" environment in the dog's digestive system;
• Avoid foods and ingredients known to produce gas;
• Avoid stressful situations for the dog, especially at mealtimes;
• Make dietary changes gradually, over a period of a few weeks;
• Do not feed dry food only;
• Although the role of genetics as a causàtive of bloat is not known, many breeders do not breed from previously affected dogs;
• Sometimes owners are advised to have gastroplexy (stomach stapling) performed on their dogs as a preventive measure.

Pay attention to your dog's behavior and any changes
that could be symptomatic of bloat. Your dog's life depends on it!

A happy Pointer on pointe!

For the Pointer's sanity (as well as that of his owner), daily exercise is the key to happiness. Any active mind is a balanced mind, especially where the Pointer is concerned. The Pointer is, by and large, one of the most active dogs any owner could choose and therefore requires considerable outdoor attention. Do not give your Pointer the opportunity to hone his destructive skills—give him plenty of activity in the yard, in the field, on the beach, etc., remembering to give plenty of rest time before and after meals.

GROOMING

Your Pointer will not demand much of your time or equipment in the way of grooming, but the dog still requires care. Regular brushing sessions keep the coat clean, odor-free and healthy. Grooming also gives you an opportunity to be aware of and treat any skin problems that might arise.

Pointers will shed their coats twice a year. Brushing is an absolute necessity at this time. Even though the Pointer's coat is short, you will be amazed at the amount of hair deposited throughout the house if a regular brushing regimen is not followed.

Regular grooming also gives you the opportunity to respond immediately to your dog's health-care needs. Such things as clipping nails, cleaning ears and brushing teeth can be taken care of during the time set aside for grooming.

Investing in a grooming table that has a non-slip top and an arm and a noose can make all of these activities infinitely easier. These tables are available at pet shops, and it is important to choose a table with a height that allows you to stand or sit comfortably while you are working on your dog. A grooming table that has an arm and a noose (to secure the dog on the table) keeps the dog from fidgeting or deciding he has had enough grooming.

Invest in a good stiff bristle brush, a steel comb and canine nail clippers or a grinder that grinds the nails down rather than actually cutting them. You will be using this equipment for many years, so buy the best equipment you can afford.

The Pointer is a natural breed with a coat that requires no clipping or trimming. This is a good time to accustom your Pointer to having his nails trimmed and having his feet inspected. Check between the toes for splinters and thorns, paying particular attention to any swollen or tender areas.

In some areas of the country, there is a weed called the fox-tail that has a barbed hook-like structure that carries its seed. This hook easily finds its way into a dog's foot or between his toes and very quickly works its way deep into the dog's flesh, causing soreness and infection. These barbs are best removed by your veterinarian before serious problems arise.

BATHING

In general, dogs need to be bathed only a few times a year, possibly more often if your dog gets into something messy or if he starts to smell like a dog. Show dogs are usually bathed before every show, which could be as frequent as weekly, although this depends on the owner. Bathing too frequently

can have negative effects on the skin and coat, removing natural oils and causing dryness.

If you give your dog his first bath when he is young, he will become accustomed to the process. Wrestling a dog into the tub or chasing a freshly shampooed dog who has escaped from the bath will be no fun! Most dogs don't naturally enjoy their baths, but you at least want yours to cooperate with you.

Before bathing the dog, have the items you'll need close at hand. First, decide where you will bathe the dog. You should have a tub or basin with a non-

Brushes come in various shapes and sizes. Select a grooming device that's comfortable for your hand.

slip surface. Puppies can even be bathed in a sink. In warm weather, some like to use a portable pool in the yard, although you'll want to make sure your dog doesn't head for the nearest dirt pile following his bath! You will also need a hose or shower spray to wet the coat thoroughly, a shampoo formulated for dogs, absorbent towels and perhaps a blow dryer. Human shampoos are too harsh for dogs' coats and will dry them out.

Before wetting the dog, give him a brush-through to remove any dead hair, dirt and mats. Make sure he is at ease in the tub and have the water at a comfort-able temperature. Begin bathing by wetting the coat all the way down to the skin. Massage in the shampoo, keeping it away from his face and eyes. Rinse him thoroughly, again avoiding the eyes and ears, as you don't want to get water into the ear canals. A thorough rinsing is important, as shampoo residue is drying and itchy to the dog. After rinsing, wrap him in a towel to absorb the initial moisture. You can finish drying with either a towel or a blow dryer on low heat, held at a safe distance from the dog. You should keep the dog indoors and away from drafts until he is completely dry.

Shield your Pointer's eyes when wetting his head. Also pay attention to not spraying water into the ears.

NAIL CLIPPING

Having their nails trimmed is not on many dogs' lists of favorite things to do. With this in mind, you will need to accustom your puppy to the procedure at a young age so that he will sit still (well, as still as he can) for his pedicures. Long nails can cause the dog's feet to spread, which is not good for him; likewise, long nails can hurt if they unintentionally scratch, not good for you.

Some dogs' nails are worn down naturally by regular walking on hard surfaces, so the frequency with which you clip depends on your individual dog. Look at his nails from time to time and clip as needed; a good way to know when it's time for a trim is if you hear your dog clicking as he walks across the floor.

There are several types of nail clippers and even electric nail-grinding tools made for dogs. First, we'll discuss using the clipper. To start, have your clipper ready and some doggie treats on hand. You want your pup to view his nail-clipping sessions in a positive light, and what better way to convince him than with food? You may want to enlist the help of an assistant to comfort the pup and offer treats as you concentrate on the clipping itself. The guillotine-type clipper is thought of by many as the easiest type to use; the nail tip

Use a strong guillotine-style clipper to give your adult Pointer's nails a trim.

is inserted into the opening, and blades on the top and bottom snip it off in one clip.

Start by grasping the pup's paw; a little pressure on the foot pad causes the nail to extend, making it easier to clip. Clip off a little at a time. If you can see the "quick," which is a blood vessel that runs through each nail, you will know how much to trim, as you do not want to cut into the quick. On that note, if you do cut the quick, which will cause bleeding, you can stem the flow of blood with a styptic pencil or other clotting agent. If you mistakenly nip the quick, do not panic or fuss, as this will cause the pup to be afraid. Simply reassure the pup, stop the bleeding and move on to the next nail. Don't be discouraged; you will become a professional canine pedicurist with practice.

You may or may not be able to see the quick, so it's best to just clip off a small bit at a time. If you see a dark dot in the center of

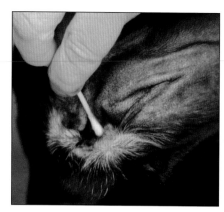

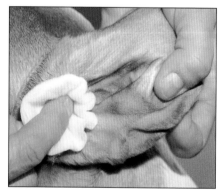

Do not forget to clean your Pointer's ears. Ask your veterinarian to show you how to do it. Rather than probing with a cotton swab (TOP), use a cotton wipe (BOTTOM), which is gentler and safer.

and there's no chance of cutting through the quick. Use the grinder on a low setting and always talk soothingly to your dog. He won't mind his salon visit, and he'll have nicely polished nails as well.

Ear Cleaning

While keeping your dog's ears clean unfortunately will not cause him to "hear" your commands any better, it will protect him from ear infection and ear-mite infestation. In addition, a dog's ears are vulnerable to waxy build-up and to collecting foreign matter from the outdoors. Look in your dog's ears regularly to ensure that they look pink, clean and otherwise healthy. Even if they look fine, an odor in the ears signals a problem and means it's time to call the vet.

the nail, this is the quick and your cue to stop clipping. Tell the puppy he's a "good boy" and offer a piece of treat with each nail. You can also use nail-clipping time to examine the footpads, making sure that they are not dry and cracked and that nothing has become embedded in them.

The nail grinder, the other choice, is many owners' first choice. Accustoming the puppy to the sound of the grinder and sensation of the buzz presents fewer challenges than the clipper,

A dog's ears should be cleaned regularly; once a week is suggested, and you can do this along with your regular brushing. Using a cotton ball or pad, and never probing into the ear canal, wipe the ear gently. You can use an ear-cleansing liquid or powder available from your vet or pet-supply store; alternatively, you might prefer to use homemade solutions with ingredients like one part white vinegar and one part hydrogen peroxide. Ask your vet about home remedies before you attempt to concoct something on your own!

Keep your dog's ears free of excess hair by plucking it as needed. If done gently, this will be painless for the dog. Look for wax, brown droppings (a sign of ear mites), redness or any other abnormalities. At the first sign of a problem, contact your vet so that he can prescribe an appropriate medication.

Eye Care

During grooming sessions, pay extra attention to the condition of your dog's eyes. If the area around the eyes is soiled or if tear staining has occurred, there are various cleaning agents made especially for this purpose. Look at the dog's eyes to make sure no debris has entered; dogs with large eyes and those who spend time outdoors are especially prone to this.

The signs of an eye infection are obvious: mucus, redness, puffiness, scabs or other signs of irritation. If your dog's eyes become infected, the vet will likely prescribe an antibiotic ointment for treatment. If you notice signs of more serious problems, such as opacities in the eye, which usually indicate cataracts, consult the vet at once. Taking time to pay attention to your dog's eyes will alert you in the early stages of any problem so that you can get your dog treatment as soon as possible. You could save your dog's sight!

A Clean Smile

Another essential part of grooming is brushing your dog's teeth and checking his overall oral condition. Studies show that around 80% of dogs experience dental problems by two years of age, and the percentage is higher in older dogs. Therefore it is highly likely that your dog will have trouble with his teeth and gums unless you are proactive with home dental care.

The most common dental problem in dogs is plaque build-up. If not treated, this causes gum disease, infection and resultant tooth loss. Bacteria from these infections spread throughout the body, affecting the vital organs. Do you need much more convincing to start brushing your dog's teeth? If so, take a good whiff of your dog's breath and read on.

Fortunately, home dental care is rather easy and convenient for pet owners. Specially formulated canine toothpaste is easy to find.

Use a soft wipe to gently clean the areas around your Pointer's eyes.

You should use one of these toothpastes, not a product for humans. Some doggie pastes are even available in flavors appealing to dogs. If your dog likes the flavor, he will tolerate the process better, making things much easier for you! Doggie toothbrushes come in different sizes and are designed to fit the contour of a canine mouth. Rubber fingertip brushes fit right on one of your fingers and have rubber nodes to clean the teeth and massage the gums. This may be easier to handle, as it is akin to rubbing your dog's teeth with your finger.

As with other grooming tasks, accustom your Pointer pup to his dental care early on. Start gently, for a few minutes at a time, so that he gets used to the feel of the brush and to your handling his mouth. Offer praise and petting so that he looks at tooth-care time as a time when he gets extra love and attention. The routine should become second nature; he may not like it, but he should at least tolerate it.

IDENTIFICATION
You love your Pointer and want to keep him safe. Of course you take every precaution to prevent his escaping from the yard or becoming lost or stolen. You have a sturdy, high fence and you always keep your dog on lead when out and about in public places. If your dog is not properly identified,

PET OR STRAY?
Besides the obvious benefit of providing your contact information to whoever finds your lost dog, an ID tag makes your dog more approachable and more likely to be recovered. A strange dog wandering the neighborhood without a collar and tags will look like a stray, while the collar and tags indicate that the dog is someone's pet. Even if the ID tags become detached from the collar, the collar alone will make a person more likely to pick up the dog.

however, you are overlooking a major aspect of his safety. We hope to never be in a situation where our dog is missing, but we should practice prevention in the unfortunate case that this happens; identification greatly increases the chances of your dog's being returned to you.

There are several ways to identify your dog. First, the traditional dog tag should be a staple in your dog's wardrobe, attached to his everyday collar. Tags can be made of sturdy plastic and various metals and should include your contact information so that a person who finds the dog can get in touch with you right away to arrange his return. Many people today enjoy the wide range of decorative tags available, so have fun and create a tag to match your dog's personality. Of course, it is important that the tag stays on the collar, so have a secure "O" ring attachment; you also can explore the type of tag that slides right onto the collar.

In addition to the ID tag, which every dog should wear even if identified by another method, two other forms of identification have become popular: microchipping and tattooing. In microchipping, a tiny scannable chip is painlessly inserted under the dog's skin. The number is registered to you so that, if your lost dog turns up at a clinic or shelter, the chip can be scanned to retrieve your contact information.

The advantage of the microchip is that it is a permanent form of ID, but there are some factors to consider. Several different companies make microchips, and not all are compatible with the others' scanning devices. It's best to find a company with a universal microchip that can be read by scanners made by other companies as well. It won't do any good to have the dog chipped if the information cannot be retrieved. Also, not every humane society, shelter and clinic is equipped with a scanner, although more and more facilities are equipping themselves. In fact, many shelters microchip dogs that they adopt out to new homes. Regardless, a tag with your contact information is always a must.

If you are going on vacation and need to board your Pointer, research boarding kennels ahead of time. Select a clean kennel with an attentive staff and enough room to allow your Pointer daily exercise.

HOUSE-TRAINING YOUR POINTER

Dogs are tactility-oriented when it comes to house-training. In other words, they respond to the surface on which they are given approval to eliminate. The choice is yours (the dog's version is in parentheses): The lawn (including the neighbors' lawns)? A bare patch of earth under a tree (where people like to sit and relax in the summertime)? Concrete steps or patio (all sidewalks, garages and basement floors)? The curbside (watch out for cars)? A small area of crushed stone in a corner of the yard (mine!)? The latter is the best choice if you can manage it

You select the area in which your Pointer is to relieve himself. Once trained, he will always return to the same spot.

because it will remain strictly for the dog's use and is easy to keep clean.

You can start out with paper-training indoors and switch over to an outdoor surface as the puppy matures and gains control over his need to eliminate. For the nay-sayers, don't worry—this won't mean that the dog will soil on every piece of newspaper lying around the house. You are training him to go outside, remember?

BASIC PRINCIPLES OF DOG TRAINING

1. Start training early. A young puppy is ready, willing and able.
2. Timing is your all-important tool. Praise at the exact time that the dog responds correctly. Pay close attention.
3. Patience is almost as important as timing!
4. Repeat! The same word has to mean the same thing every time.
5. In the beginning, praise all correct behavior verbally, along with treats and petting.

WHEN YOUR PUPPY'S "GOT TO GO"
Your puppy's need to relieve himself is seemingly non-stop, but signs of improvement will be seen each week. From 8 to 10 weeks old, the puppy will have to be taken outside every time he wakes up, about 10–15 minutes after every meal and after every period of play—all day long, from first thing in the morning until his bedtime! That's a total of ten or more trips per day to teach the puppy where it's okay to relieve himself. With that schedule in mind, you can see that house-training a young puppy is not a part-time job. It requires someone to be home all day.

If that seems overwhelming or impossible, do a little planning. For example, plan to pick up your puppy at the start of a vacation period. If you can't get home in the middle of the day, plan to hire a dog-sitter or ask a neighbor to come over to take the pup outside, feed him his lunch and then take him out again about ten or so minutes after he's eaten. Also make arrangements with that or another person to be your "emergency" contact if you have to stay late on the job. Remind yourself—repeatedly—that this hectic schedule improves as the puppy gets older.

HOME WITHIN A HOME
Your Pointer puppy needs to be confined to one secure, puppy-proof area when no one is able to watch his every move. Generally the kitchen is the place of choice because the floor is washable. Likewise, it's a busy family area that will accustom the pup to a variety of noises, everything from pots and pans to the telephone, blender and dishwasher. He will also be enchanted by the smell of your cooking (and will never be critical when you burn something). A sturdy exercise pen (also called an "ex-pen," a puppy version of a playpen) with sufficiently high sides is a helpful tool in confining a young pup. Placed within the room of choice, the pen allows the pup to see out and has a certain amount of space

POTTY COMMAND

Most dogs love to please their masters; there are no bounds to what dogs will do to make their owners happy. The potty command is a good example of this theory. If toileting on command makes the master happy, then more power to him. Puppies will obligingly piddle if it really makes their keepers smile. Some owners can be creative about which word they will use to command their dogs to relieve themselves. Some popular choices are "Potty," "Tinkle," "Piddle," "Let's go," "Hurry up" and "Toilet." Give the command every time your puppy goes into position and the puppy will begin to associate his business with the command.

Once housebroken, your Pointer will let you know when he needs to "go out." Learn to recognize the signs.

provides. How often have you seen adult dogs that choose to sleep under a table or chair even though they have full run of the house? It's the den connection.

In your "happy" voice, use the word "Crate" every time you put the pup into his den. If he's new to a crate, toss in a small biscuit for him to chase the first few times. At night, after he's been outside, he should sleep in his crate. The crate may be kept in his designated area at night or, if you want to be sure to hear those wake-up yips in the morning, put the crate in a corner of your bedroom. However, don't make any response whatsoever to

in which he can run about, but he is safe from dangerous things like electrical cords, heating units, trash baskets or open kitchen-supply cabinets. Place the pen where the puppy will not get a blast of heat or air conditioning.

In the pen, you can put a few toys, his bed (which can be his crate if the dimensions of pen and crate are compatible) and a few layers of newspaper in one small corner, just in case. A water bowl can be hung at a convenient height on the side of the ex-pen so it won't become a splashing pool for an innovative puppy. His food dish can go on the floor, next to the water bowl.

Crates are something that pet owners are at last getting used to for their dogs. Wild or domestic canines have always preferred to sleep in den-like safe spots, and that is exactly what the crate

> **EXTRA! EXTRA!**
> The headlines read: "Puppy Piddles Here!" Breeders commonly use newspapers to line their whelping pens, so puppies learn to associate newspapers with relieving themselves. Do not use newspapers to line your pup's crate, as this will signal to your puppy that it is OK to urinate in his crate. If you choose to paper-train your puppy, you will layer newspapers on a section of the floor near the door he uses to go outside. You should encourage the puppy to use the papers to relieve himself, and bring him there whenever you see him getting ready to go. Little by little, you will reduce the size of the newspaper-covered area so that the puppy will learn to relieve himself "on the other side of the door."

whining or crying. If he's completely ignored, he'll settle down and get to sleep.

Good bedding for a young puppy is an old folded bath towel or an old blanket, something that is easily washable and disposable if necessary ("accidents" will happen!). Never put newspaper in the puppy's crate. Also those old ideas about adding a clock to replace his mother's heartbeat, or a hot-water bottle to replace her warmth, are just that—old ideas. The clock could drive the puppy nuts, and the hot-water bottle could end up as a very soggy waterbed! An extremely good breeder would have introduced your puppy to the crate by letting two pups sleep together for a couple of nights, followed by several nights alone. How thankful you will be if you found that breeder!

Safe toys in the pup's crate or area will keep him occupied, but monitor their condition closely. Discard any toys that show signs of being chewed to bits. Squeaky parts, bits of stuffing or plastic or any other small pieces can cause intestinal blockage or possibly choking if swallowed.

PROGRESSING WITH POTTY-TRAINING
After you've taken your puppy out and he has relieved himself in the area you've selected, he can have some free time with the family as long as there is someone

Although Pointers aren't known to be master chefs, the kitchen is certainly their favorite room. Most owners choose to puppy-proof and confine the pup to this general area until house-training is complete.

responsible for watching him. That doesn't mean just someone in the same room who is watching TV or busy on the computer, but one person who is doing nothing other than keeping an eye on the pup, playing with him on the floor and helping him understand his position in the pack.

This first taste of freedom will let you begin to set the house rules. If you don't want the dog on the furniture, now is the time to prevent his first attempts to jump up onto the couch. The word to use in this case is "Off," not "Down." "Down" is the word you will use to teach the down position, which is something entirely different.

Most corrections at this stage

Kinnike Lynda, shown at four weeks of age. Very young puppies need to relieve themselves often and have little control. Their control, of course, improves with age and training.

come in the form of simply distracting the puppy. Instead of telling him "No" for "Don't chew the carpet," distract the chomping puppy with a toy and he'll forget about the carpet.

As you are playing with the pup, do not forget to watch him closely and pay attention to his body language. Whenever you see him begin to circle or sniff, take the puppy outside to relieve himself. If you are paper-training, put him back into his confined area on the newspapers. In either case, praise him as he eliminates while he actually is in the act of relieving himself. Three seconds after he has finished is too late! You'll be praising him for running toward you, or picking up a toy or whatever he may be doing at that moment, and that's not what you want to be praising him for. Timing is a vital tool in all dog training. Use it.

Remove soiled newspapers

immediately and replace them with clean ones. You may want to take a small piece of soiled paper and place it in the middle of the new clean papers, as the scent will attract him to that spot when it's time to go again. That scent attraction is why it's so important to clean up any messes made in the house by using a product specially made to eliminate the odor of dog urine and droppings. Regular household cleansers won't do the trick. Pet shops sell the best pet deodorizers. Invest in the largest container you can find.

Scent attraction eventually will lead your pup to his chosen spot outdoors; this is the basis of outdoor training. When you take your puppy outside to relieve

TIDY BOY

Clean by nature, dogs do not like to soil their dens, which in effect are their crates or sleeping quarters. Unless not feeling well, dogs will not defecate or urinate in their crates. Crate training capitalizes on the dog's natural desire to keep his den clean. Be conscientious about giving the puppy as many opportunities to relieve himself outdoors as possible. Reward the puppy for correct behavior. Praise him and pat him whenever he "goes" in the correct location. Even the tidiest of puppies can have potty accidents, so be patient and dedicate more energy to helping your puppy achieve a clean lifestyle.

himself, use a one-word command such as "Outside" or "Go-potty" (that's one word to the puppy!) as you pick him up and attach his leash. Then put him down in his area. If he is too big for you to carry, snap the leash on quickly and lead him to his spot. Now comes the hard part—hard for you, that is. Just stand there until he urinates and defecates. Move him a few feet in one direction or another if he's just sitting there looking at you, but remember that this is neither playtime nor time for a walk. This is strictly a business trip! Then, as he circles and squats (remember your timing!), give him a quiet "Good dog" as praise. If you start to jump for joy, ecstatic over his performance, he'll do one of two things: either he will stop mid-stream, as it were, or he'll do it again for you—in the house—and expect you to be just as delighted!

Give him five minutes or so and, if he doesn't go in that time, take him back indoors to his confined area and try again in another ten minutes, or immediately if you see him sniffing and circling. By careful observation, you'll soon work out a successful schedule.

Accidents, by the way, are just that—accidents. Clean them up quickly and thoroughly, without comment, after the puppy has been taken outside to finish his business and then put back into his area or crate. If you witness an accident in progress, say "No!" in a stern voice and get the pup outdoors immediately. No punishment is needed. You and your puppy are just learning each other's language, and sometimes it's easy to miss a puppy's

DAILY SCHEDULE
How many relief trips does your puppy need per day? A puppy up to the age of 14 weeks will need to go outside about 8 to 12 times per day! You will have to take the pup out any time he starts sniffing around the floor or turning in small circles, as well as after naps, meals, games and lessons or whenever he's released from his crate. Once the puppy is 14 to 22 weeks of age, he will require only 6 to 8 relief trips. At the ages of 22 to 32 weeks, the puppy will require about 5 to 7 trips. Adult dogs typically require 4 relief trips per day, in the morning, afternoon, evening and late at night.

LEASH TRAINING

House-training and leash training go hand in hand, literally. When taking your puppy outside to do his business, lead him there on his leash. Unless an emergency potty run is called for, do not whisk the puppy up into your arms and take him outside. If you have a fenced yard, you have the advantage of letting the puppy loose to go out, but it's better to put the dog on the leash and take him to his designated place in the yard until he is reliably house-trained. Taking the puppy for a walk is the best way to house-train a dog. The dog will associate the walk with his time to relieve himself, and the exercise of walking stimulates the dog's bowels and bladder. Dogs that are not trained to relieve themselves on a walk may hold it until they get back home, which of course defeats half the purpose of the walk.

message. Chalk it up to experience and watch more closely from now on.

COLLAR AND LEASH

If your Pointer is a pet or show puppy, he must be used to his collar and leash. We'll see that hunting kids sometimes start out with a check cord before the collar. Choose a collar for your puppy that is secure but not heavy or bulky. He won't enjoy training if he's uncomfortable. A flat buckle collar is fine for everyday wear and for initial puppy training. For older dogs, there are several types of training collars such as the martingale, which is a double loop that tightens slightly around the neck, or the head collar, which is similar to a horse's halter. Do not use a chain choke collar unless you have been specifically shown how to put it on and how to use it. You may not be disposed to use a chain choke collar even if your breeder has told you that it's suitable for your Pointer.

A lightweight 6-foot woven cotton or nylon training leash is preferred by most trainers because it is easy to fold up in your hand and comfortable to hold because there is a certain amount of give to it. There are lessons where the dog will start off 6 feet away from you at the end of the leash. The leash used to take the puppy outside to relieve himself is shorter because you don't want him to roam away from his area. The shorter leash will also be the one to use when you walk the puppy.

If you've been wise enough to enroll in a puppy kindergarten training class, suggestions will be made as to the best collar and leash for your young puppy. I say "wise" because your puppy will be in a class with puppies in his age range (up to five months old) of all breeds and sizes. It's the perfect way for him to learn the right way (and the wrong way) to interact with other dogs as well as their people. You cannot teach your puppy how to interpret another dog's sign language. For a first-time puppy owner, these socialization classes are invaluable. For experienced dog owners, they are a real boon to further training.

EXERCISES FOR A BASIC CANINE EDUCATION

THE SIT EXERCISE

There are several ways to teach the puppy to sit. The first one is to catch him whenever he is about to sit and, as his backside nears the floor, say "Sit, good dog!" That's positive reinforcement and, if your timing is sharp, he will learn that what he's doing at that second is connected to your saying "Sit" and that you think he's clever for doing it!

Another method is to start with the puppy on his leash in front of you. Show him a treat in the palm of your right hand. Bring your hand up under his nose and, almost in slow motion, move your hand up and back so his nose goes up in the air and his head tilts back as he follows the treat in your hand. At that point, he will have to either sit or fall over, so as his back legs buckle under, say "Sit, good dog," and then give him the treat and lots of praise. You may have to begin with your hand lightly running up his chest,

actually lifting his chin up until he sits. Some (usually older) dogs require gentle pressure on their hindquarters with the left hand, in which case the dog should be on your left side. Puppies generally do not appreciate this physical dominance.

After a few times, you should be able to show the dog a treat in the open palm of your hand, raise your hand waist-high as you say "Sit" and have him sit. Once again, you have taught him two things at the same time. Both the verbal command and the motion of the hand are signals for the sit. Your puppy is watching you

Teaching the sit is the most basic command and the first you will teach your Pointer. Sometimes you may have to guide the dog into the proper position until he is familiar with it.

THE DOWN EXERCISE

Before beginning to teach the down command, you must consider how the dog feels about this exercise. To him, "down" is a submissive position. Being flat on the floor with you standing over him is not his idea of fun. It's up to you to let him know that, while it may not be fun, the reward of your approval is worth his effort.

Start with the puppy on your left side in a sit position. Hold the leash right above his collar in your left hand. Have an extra-special treat, such as a small piece of cooked chicken or hot dog, in your right hand. Place it at the end of the pup's nose and steadily move your hand down and forward along the ground. Hold the leash to prevent a sudden lunge for the food. As the puppy goes into the down position, say "Down" very gently.

The difficulty with this exercise is twofold: it's both the submissive aspect and the fact that most people say the word "Down" as if they were drill sergeants in charge of recruits! So issue the command sweetly, give him the treat and have the pup maintain the down position for several seconds. If he tries to get up immediately, place your hands on his shoulders and press down gently, giving him a very quiet "Good dog." As you progress with this lesson, increase the "down time" until he will hold it until you say "Okay" (his cue for

almost more than he is listening to you, so what you do is just as important as what you say.

Don't save any of these drills only for training sessions. Use them as much as possible at odd times during a normal day. The dog should always sit before being given his food dish. He should sit to let you go through a doorway first, when the doorbell rings or when you stop to speak to someone on the street.

> ## "SCHOOL" MODE
> When is your puppy ready for a lesson? Maybe not always when you are. Attempting training with treats just before his mealtime is asking for disaster. Notice what times of day he performs best and make that Fido's school time.

release). Practice this one in the house at various times throughout the day.

By increasing the length of time during which the dog must maintain the down position, you'll find many uses for it. For example, he can lie at your feet in the vet's office or anywhere that both of you have to wait, when you are on the phone, while the family is eating and so forth. If you progress to training for competitive obedience, he'll already be all set for the exercise called the "long down."

THE STAY EXERCISE

You can teach your Pointer to stay in the sit, down and stand positions. To teach the sit/stay, have the dog sit on your left side. Hold the leash at waist level in your left hand, and let the dog know that you have a treat in your closed right hand. Step forward on your right foot as you say "Stay." Immediately turn and stand directly in front of the dog, keeping your right hand up high so he'll keep his eye on the treat hand and maintain the sit position for a count of five. Return to your original position and offer the reward.

Increase the length of the sit/stay each time until the dog can hold it for at least 30 seconds without moving. After about a week of success, move out on your right foot and take two steps

before turning to face the dog. Give the "Stay" hand signal (left palm back, facing the dog's head) as you leave. He gets the treat when you return and he holds the sit/stay. Increase the distance that you walk away from him before turning until you reach the length of your training leash. But don't rush it! Go back to the beginning if he moves before he should. No matter what the lesson, never be upset by having to back up for a few days. The repetition and practice are what will make your dog reliable in these commands. It

Always introduce new lessons with the dog on lead. Here, a Pointer and his owner practice the sit/stay.

won't do any good to move on to something more difficult if the command is not mastered at the easier levels. Above all, even if you do get frustrated, never let your puppy know! Always keep a positive, upbeat attitude during training, which will transmit to your dog for positive results.

The down/stay is taught in the same way once the dog is completely reliable and steady with the down command. Again, don't rush it. With the dog in the down position on your left side, step out on your right foot as you say "Stay." Return by walking around in back of the dog and into your original position. While you are training, it's okay to murmur something like "Hold on" to encourage him to stay put. When the dog will stay without moving when you are at a distance of 3 or 4 feet, begin to increase the length of time before

A fenced yard is a must for the active Pointer. For your dog's safety, off-leash training and exercise should only be done in an enclosed area.

> ### COME AND GET IT!
> The come command is your dog's safety signal. Until he is 99% perfect in responding, don't use the come command if you cannot enforce it. Practice on leash with treats or squeakers, or whenever the dog is running to you. Never call him to come to you if he is to be corrected for a misdemeanor. Reward the dog with a treat and happy praise whenever he comes to you.

you return. Be sure he holds the down on your return until you say "Okay." At that point, he gets his treat—just so he'll remember for next time that it's not over until it's over.

THE COME/HERE EXERCISE
No command is more important to the safety of your Pointer than "Come" (or "Here" for the field puppy, discussed later). It is what you should say every single time you see the puppy running toward you: "Bentley, come! Good dog." During playtime, run a few feet away from the puppy and turn and tell him to "Come" as he is already running to you. You can go so far as to teach your puppy two things at once if you squat down and hold out your arms. As the pup gets close to you and you're saying "Good dog," bring your right arm in about waist high. Now he's also learning the

hand signal, an excellent device should you be on the phone when you need to get him to come to you! You'll also both be one step ahead when you enter obedience classes.

When the puppy responds to your well-timed "Come," try it with the puppy on the training leash. This time, catch him off-guard, while he's sniffing a leaf or watching a bird: "Bentley, come!" Teaching a reliable come is a challenge for owners of curious Pointers. You may have to pause for a split second after his name to be sure you have his attention. If the puppy shows any sign of confusion, give the leash a mild jerk and take a couple of steps backward. Do not repeat the command. In this case, you should say "Good come" as he reaches you.

That's the number-one rule of training. Each command word is given just once. Anything more is nagging. You'll also notice that all commands are one word only. Even when they are actually two words, you say them as one.

Never call the dog to come to you—with or without his name— if you are angry or intend to correct him for some misbehavior. When correcting the pup, you go to him. Your dog must always connect "Come" with something pleasant and with your approval; then you can rely on his response.

Puppies, like children, have

notoriously short attention spans, so don't overdo it with any of the training. Keep each lesson short. Break it up with a quick run around the yard or a ball toss, repeat the lesson and quit as soon as the pup gets it right. That way, you will always end with a "Good dog."

Life isn't perfect and neither are puppies. A time will come, often around ten months of age, when he'll become "selectively deaf" or choose to "forget" his name. He may respond by wagging his tail (and even seeming to smile at you) with a look that says "Make me!" Laugh, throw his favorite toy and skip the lesson you had planned.

Incorporate a game of fetch into your Pointer's come exercise. Your Pointer must obey the come command at all times.

THE HEEL EXERCISE
The second most important command to teach, after the come, is the heel. When you are walking your growing puppy, you need to

be in control. Besides, it looks terrible to be pulled and yanked down the street, and it's not much fun either. Your eight- to ten-week-old puppy will probably follow you everywhere, but that's

THE HEEL COMMAND WITH A POINTER

If your puppy is to be only a pet or show dog, teaching the heel command is essential. For hunting puppies, this lesson can be postponed until the dog responds reliably to the whoa command (even in the fluttery presence of distracting pigeons) and has been worked on the check cord for a period of a few months. Some hunting Pointers don't begin formal heel work until they are one year of age.

his natural instinct, not your control over the situation. However, any time he does follow you, you can say "Heel" and be ahead of the game, as he will learn to associate this command with the action of following you before you even begin teaching him to heel.

There is a very precise, almost military, procedure for teaching your dog to heel. As with all other obedience training, begin with the dog on your left side. He will be in a very nice sit and you will have the training leash across your chest. Hold the loop and folded leash in your right hand. Pick up the slack leash above the dog in your left hand and hold it loosely at your side. Step out on your left foot as you say "Heel." If the puppy does not move, give a gentle tug or pat your left leg to get him started. If he surges ahead of you, stop and pull him back gently until he is at your side. Tell him to sit and begin again.

Walk a few steps and stop while the puppy is correctly beside you. Tell him to sit and give mild verbal praise. (More enthusiastic praise will encourage him to think the lesson is over.) Repeat the lesson, increasing the number of steps you take only as long as the dog is heeling nicely beside you. When you end the lesson, have him hold the sit, then give him the "Okay" to let him know that this is the end of the lesson. Praise him so that he knows he did a good job.

The cure for excessive pulling (a common problem) is to stop when the dog is no more than 2 or 3 feet ahead of you. Guide him back into position and begin again. With a really determined puller, try switching to a head collar. This will automatically turn the pup's head toward you so you can bring him back easily to the heel position. Give quiet, reassuring praise every time the leash goes slack and he's staying with you.

Staying and heeling can take a lot out of a dog, so provide playtime and free-running exercise to shake off the stress when the lessons are over. You don't want him to associate training with all work and no fun.

TRAINING YOUR POINTER PUPPY FOR FIELD WORK

Training a gundog puppy for hunting is not unlike training a puppy for basic obedience: first and foremost you must gain the puppy's respect and trust. And you do this through the puppy's most vital organ: his nose, which in the Pointer is attached directly to his second most vital organ, his stomach. Use treats and lots of them, the smellier the better. And what goes down best with liver? You guessed it: praise, praise, praise. Positive reinforcement is the road to take with training a Pointer.

You can learn about training gundogs by reading books on the subject, by attending a gun club's classes for hunting tests or seminars hosted by professional trainers and/or by hiring a professional trainer. All of these are legitimate avenues to pursue, each of them leading to the same end result: becoming smarter than your puppy. With the Pointer puppy, you have to contend not only with the breed's intelligence and strong instincts but also with his high prey drive and his unbeatable nose. Look at the photos in this book: how large is the adult Pointer's nose!

If your goal with your Pointer puppy is to have a reliably trained companion on a weekend hunt, and not to compete for prizes in a field trial, then a professional trainer is probably not necessary. The critical word to remember is "companion," and your Pointer is primarily your pet. You'll spend

The Pointer's instinctive traits must be taken into account when undertaking training.

much more time with this dog inside the home and horsing around in the back yard than you will out in the field. Competitive field trials are a completely different pursuit, and these events require much more time and money than does a weekend hunting trip. Furthermore, dogs trained for field trials are expected to work flawlessly for long hours, never missing a blind retrieve or breaking concentration.

Your puppy's education should start at around eight to ten weeks of age, which is usually the time that the puppy comes to his new home. Don't wait until the puppy is six months old or beyond. The puppy doesn't need to enjoy every moment of his puppyhood at home with mom and the kids: he needs to get his paws and nose into the field. The most critical period in training a hunting puppy is the first 12

months, and you must commit to make the most of this if you want your puppy to become a proficient field dog. When the puppy is three months old, he should already be learning basic commands and enjoying the fun of being out in the field with his human pal.

Encourage your puppy to love everything about the hunt. Do not admonish your Pointer for scurrying away with the bumper or chasing a quail in the wrong direction. Keep the training realistic. Your first Pointer puppy is not going to be the youngest Field Champion in UKC history or qualify for Amateur All-Age before he's finished growing. Your goals for the young puppy are simple: to make hunting enjoyable and teach the puppy to respond to the command "Here" or "Come." These are two critical lessons in the life of any hunting dog. Don't pressure your puppy or expect too much too soon. You don't want your Pointer puppy to become a worrier, unable to focus on the lesson or to enjoy the time he's spending with you. Stress has ruined many potential greats, even those that were destined to become field trial winners of great style, speed and range.

Along the same lines, it's worth mentioning that shock collars don't really fit the bill for any form of introductory or casual training. These devices, when

There is no doubt about the Pointer's natural athleticism and boundless energy.

used properly, can correct a dog who is willfully disobedient, but they do little more than to stress and depress young dogs just learning the ropes.

Bird dogs excel when they're happy and doing what pleases you. Give your puppy time to express his natural talents and instincts. Less pressure is better when first training the puppy. If you watch your puppy carefully, he'll give you signs that he understands, is processing the lesson and is prepared to obey. Zapping a confused puppy, who's unable to decipher your commands, is cruel and stupid. Commit yourself to training your hunting companion. This partnership requires time, attention, money, effort, study and more. The rewards of this association are ineffable: ask any hunter and he'll tell you that for a few hours.

The basic equipment you will need for hunt training includes a whistle and a proper collar (or check cord).

HUNTING PUPPY'S LESSON PLAN

As mentioned, the first year of your Pointer puppy's life is critical, and our lesson plan begins at eight weeks of age. Playing with the pup makes a great start, as you can teach the puppy to retrieve a ball or another toy. Within a couple of weeks you can introduce other "toys" to the game, like a wooden dowel, a decoy, a bumper, a dummy, etc. Socialization, of course, is important for every puppy: expose him to different environments, noises, people and other animals. You can't predict when you'll teach his first lesson (regardless of which one) since you will start using it within minutes of the puppy's arrival. "No!" is more than an exclamation, it's a command and it means that the puppy must pay attention to you and stop doing whatever he's engaged in. When you use the no command, be sure to give the puppy a toy or a task or anything fun so that even the negative command becomes positive. After you give the pup his toy, praise profusely for doing the correct thing. Puppies don't know how to just stop. Practice the "No" command over the next few months.

As a part of house-training, you'll introduce the puppy to his

The hunter attaches a bell to the Pointer's collar to help keep track of the dog. While the dog is moving and working the bell rings, but when the dog freezes on point, the bell stops. This is the hunter's signal to go to his dog and flush and kill the game.

crate, and you will use the command "Crate" (or "Kennel") every time you open the door and scoot your puppy inside. The first few times, you can toss a tiny goodie into the crate to encourage him to scramble in. In no time at all, he'll recognize what you want. You will also introduce a light puppy collar, which makes the puppy a bit more controllable at this young age. This is not his training collar, which comes much later.

By the time the puppy is three months of age, you'll want to attach a lead to that collar and take the puppy on short walks. This is just a casual exercise and not the beginning of the heel command. Keep exercise moderate at this stage, though you can lengthen the walks by the time the puppy is four months old.

Spend lots of time with the puppy, teaching him the come command, sometimes called the "here." Get down on all fours and call the puppy to you. Every time he comes, you should praise him with petting and happy talk. You want your puppy to live to please you, and praise is your best method.

By four months of age, it's YMCA time: swimming lessons! Introduce the puppy to a calm body of water, preferably a clean lake or a river at low tide. Only do this in the spring or summer when the water is temperate, since puppies don't like jumping into cold, icy water any more than you do! Let the puppy get used to the water's edge. Don't rush him, as you don't want to frighten the puppy and make him afraid of the water. Once he's comfortable around the edge, walk out a short distance and encourage the puppy to follow. Being close to you should be all the encouragement he needs. Throw a bumper into the water to encourage him to go after it; don't expect him to retrieve it just yet. If you have an older dog or a friend who has a well-behaved retriever, bring them along one day. Dogs learn by watching, and it's a lot easier for a dog to learn from a four-legged friend in the water than from his dog-paddling master.

By five months of age, your puppy should be learning his basic commands, including the sit. You can reinforce these daily with a couple of ten-minute lessons. Once you feel confident that the puppy comprehends and obeys the sit, you can introduce the whistle to the command (one toot indicates sit). For field dogs, the sit command is a handy one; it's helpful to give the command to the dog so that he will sit quietly while you prepare to shoot or approach game. It's an advantage, and the dog's obedience is a great plus.

Next you teach the whoa command, which is gundog talk for "stay." This command is a natural extension of the sit

exercise. It is used primarily in the field but can be handy in other situations as well. (By the way, some owners opt to teach the whoa command earlier in pup's life, rather than waiting until five or six months.) For example, say "Whoa" just before releasing pup from his crate or before letting him out the door or into the car. Use the leash for gentle restraint when teaching the whoa. In practicing all of these commands, never let the individual training sessions exceed 20 minutes; keep them shorter if you see signs of boredom or resistance. Your Pointer will learn best if he is eager and having fun.

Instead of using the leash and collar on your puppy, you should begin to rely on the check cord, which is a 12-foot light line that attaches around the dog's neck. He should get used to dragging the cord around him. In effect, this becomes your life line: you can rely on it to enforce your commands in the yard, in the

Experienced hunters often use beeper collars when working in the field.

At five or six months of age, the Pointer is introduced to game. The hunter must keep his Pointer under control at all times.

dummies or bumpers. The intention here is to ignite the puppy's desire to chase, what Pointer folk call the prey drive.

Certainly by the time your Pointer puppy is five or six months of age, you will know him well enough to realize that he's a very driven little guy (or gal) and that his hunting instincts are nearly irrepressible. Now it's time to ignite his prey drive by introducing your bird dog to his namesake: the bird. An average-sized cold dead pigeon, quail or chukar will do nicely. Your puppy should be restrained on his leash when you introduce the bird to him. Allow him to sniff it but not to get too crazy with it. You don't want to encourage mishandling, so be ready to correct him. After a few times, the puppy should be handling the bird correctly.

By the time he's seven months of age, you will be exposing the puppy to gunfire, which should be a happy, fun sound to the puppy, not a scary, intimidating one. Give the puppy a pigeon so that he's in prey-drive mode, and then have someone fire a gun (a training pistol…a shotgun would terrify a pup) on the opposite side of the property (at least 100 feet away). Praise the puppy for ignoring the sound or for wagging his tail and continuing to carry his prize bird. The next time you do this exercise, have the gun fired at a closer range. Within a

living room and in the field. At around four or five months you'll begin taking the puppy afield with the check cord and introducing some simple retrieves. At this stage, you use

week or two, the puppy won't mind the gun being fired within a few feet of him.

When working with the puppy, keep the check cord on him, especially as you're beginning to take him in the field with you. The cord will afford you the control you need to enforce the commands you've taught thus far. Practice these commands in a variety of settings, with distractions and temptations, so that the Pointer puppy has no hesitation before obeying the command. Executing the come in your back yard is a no-brainer, but try commanding the puppy to come while he's busy sniffing at cover in the field!

This brings us to the subject of cover. It's time for the puppy to recognize that all dead pigeons don't come out of the freezer. Hide a pigeon in low cover and encourage the puppy to locate it. He'll use his nose, which is more than ample. Take the puppy to areas that abound with birds so that he can fill his nose with feathery wonder. All this makes him aware that pigeons and other fowl can be found in natural cover, and now he'll start sniffing around every time he nears cover. It's always a wonder when you see your puppy on his first point: just naturally standing there frozen in that emblematic position. When you know that your puppy is reliable on the whoa command when there are birds present, you know you've made true and meaningful progress.

Once out in the field, the trained Pointer slips into prey-drive mode. The bright orange collar helps the owner see his Pointer in heavy cover.

Here's a seasoned hunter with his nose full of "bird."

At about the seven-month mark, you can step up your puppy's exercise by giving him more time for free running, swimming or even light jogging alongside his master. (Are you ready for this?) For this type of exercise, your dog should use a harness instead of the collar and leash.

From the age of six to nine months, you're spending as much time as possible with your puppy, getting him in shape, molding his instincts and filling his nose with all things bird. And since your little guy is growing up—he's not so little by nine months—you'll see that he's developing into a real athletic hunter who is biddable and attentive. By nine months of age, he will be steady on wing once he's pointed the game. You'll also see that he has developed true purpose when you take him into the field. He may even begin to retrieve the bird by this time, but it's not necessary to pressure him into doing so. Until the puppy is a year old, you will continue to work with him in the field with the check cord.

HUNTING POINTERS FOR YOUR POINTER

When working with your hunting puppy on the check cord, the here command is a great place to start. The check cord necessarily acts like a fishing pole: you can reel your Pointer in whenever you're ready. Call out "Here!" to your puppy to get him to come to you, and when he gets to you give him lots of praise. If he doesn't come straightaway, reel him in and praise him all the same. It's a fun game for the puppy and functions to teach the puppy that coming to you is a good thing. Practice this at various times every day, first in the back yard and then in the field. You also can start teaching the here command in the house

WHISTLE WHILE YOU WORK

Practice the here (come) command in the field with your puppy. The field presents many obstacles and distractions to the puppy, which is why it's so important to practice commands in the field once the puppy is reliably responding to them in the yard. Now is the time to begin overlaying whistle commands with the here. Eventually you will be able to use the whistle command alone without the vocal reinforcement.

from day one, using the word when releasing puppy from his crate, when offering his food bowl, with games and when on those puppy walks. The opportunities are endless.

Training the Pointer to come (whether to "Come" or "Here") presents a challenge to many owners, largely due to the breed's strong prey drive. Pointers are among the most focused gundogs in the family, and sometimes their "singleness of mind" (a.k.a. thick-headedness) can be difficult to re-direct toward obedience work. Therefore, you have to hammer home to your puppy that obeying commands instantly is the most rewarding thing in the world—even more rewarding than chasing a stray skunk or wayward pigeon.

One method of reinforcing this kind of training is through distraction work. You set your puppy up to locate a bird under cover. Once he's getting close and driving toward it, give him the here command. If he doesn't obey right away, reel him in. It's rare to find a Pointer puppy who will instantly obey in this situation. Practice this scenario for a month (or two) in order to gain complete obedience from your puppy. You can start this with a puppy once he's five or six months of age.

The Pointer is infamous for being the "fair weather" gundog, meaning that he only wants to obey you on sunny days.

Don't forget to keep hunting fun and enjoyable for your Pointer student. He has to love his job in the field.

Consistency is the key in training the (stubborn, persistent, difficult) Pointer puppy. Many owners who hunt confess that their dogs are perfect students at home, but once in the field they have a mind (and a nose) all their own. Obedience in the field is the point, so you can't compromise. You must insist on correct responses at home, in the yard and in the field—even when you don't feel like enforcing the no, whoa or here command. Here are a few hints for training: first, don't give the command if you're not going to follow up; second, give the command once, not twice or 44 times or else your Pointer puppy will wait till you're in the 40s to respond; third, don't put your gun before your dog, meaning hunting is a pleasure you share with your well-trained dog and sometimes you have to sacrifice hunting time for training time.

Keep your puppy motivated and he will master anything. Let your puppy get absorbed into the excitement of the hunt. Don't keep distracting him with commands and tugging at his check cord. You'll wear him down if you over-handle him in the field or he'll become anxious and won't perform.

Practice commands in the field before attempting to hunt with your Pointer.

Don't give commands to the dog unless you can see him and reel him in if necessary. If you're giving more than one command per hour, you're overdoing it. Relax, it's supposed to be fun for you and the dog!

Many Pointer folk confess that sometimes you just can't fight the dog's instincts. Pointers can be thick-headed, with their whole mentality ruled by the nose on the end of their dish face. Surely a twitch in the cover and the irresistible scent of quail hold far more allure than the master's tooting "Yankee Doodle" in his whistle. And who can mistake the Pointer's facial expression for "Just a minute, will ya?"

Great hunting dogs are the product of home dedication, or more specifically back yard dedication. You have to start with your pup at home in your yard and gain control of him. Practicing at home is key, just as repetition is critical to success in training gundogs. You don't practice on the field while you're shooting over an out-of-control young Pointer. That's not practice, that's chaos! No matter how well bred your Pointer puppy, if you can't control him, he's worthless as a bird dog. Be patient: once you've practiced enough, you'll get "in the game." One distinct advantage of working your Pointer puppy in

Keep the puppy motivated and happy. Every Pointer must be a full-time companion and faithful friend.

your back yard is the fence. The puppy learns that you are in control and that he cannot escape. Teaching the puppy to stay in close range can be more easily accomplished in the yard than in the field. Even if he stays too close—like sitting on your boots—you can fix that once you're in the field.

Remember that your Pointer puppy should become your longtime companion, someone who brings you more than your dinner in his soft mouth: he brings you great happiness and satisfaction. What more could you want from a faithful, devoted pal?

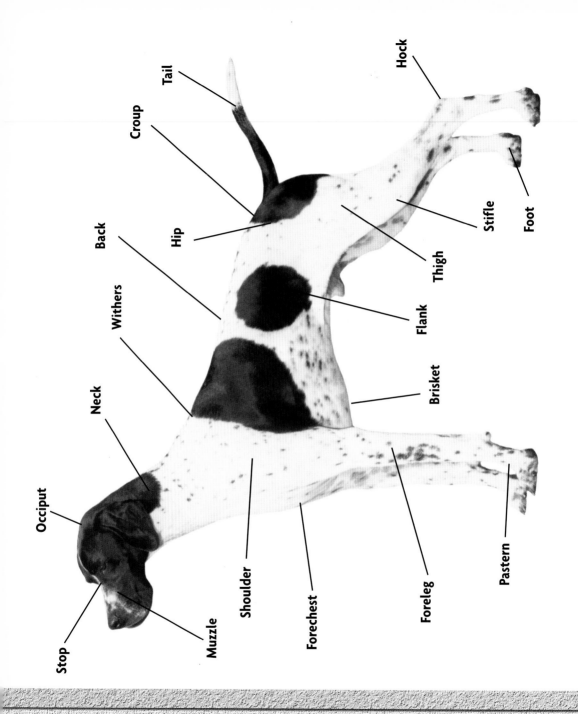

PHYSICAL STRUCTURE OF THE POINTER

Tail

Croup

Hock

Back

Hip

Stifle

Withers

Foot

Thigh

Neck

Flank

Occiput

Brisket

Stop

Muzzle

Shoulder

Forechest

Foreleg

Pastern

HEALTHCARE OF YOUR

POINTER

By Lowell Ackerman, DVM, DACVD

HEALTHCARE FOR A LIFETIME

When you own a dog, you become his healthcare advocate over his entire lifespan, as well as being the one to shoulder the financial burden of such care. Accordingly, it is worthwhile to focus on prevention rather than treatment, as you and your pet will both be happier.

Of course, the best place to have begun your program of preventive healthcare is with the initial purchase or adoption of your dog. There is no way of guaranteeing that your new furry friend is free of medical problems, but there are some things you can do to improve your odds. You certainly should have done adequate research into the Pointer and have selected your puppy carefully rather than buying on impulse. Health issues aside, a large number of pet abandonment and relinquishment cases arise from a mismatch between pet needs and owner expectations. This is entirely preventable with appropriate planning and finding a good breeder.

Regarding healthcare issues specifically, it is very difficult to make blanket statements about where to acquire a problem-free pet, but, again, a reputable breeder is your best bet. In an ideal situation you have the opportunity to see both parents, get references from other owners of the breeder's pups and see genetic-testing documentation for several generations of the litter's ancestors. At the very least, you must thoroughly investigate the Pointer and the problems inherent in that breed, as well as the genetic testing available to screen for those problems. Genetic testing offers some important benefits, but testing is available for only a few disorders in a relatively small number of breeds and is not available for some of the most common genetic diseases, such as hip dysplasia, cataracts, epilepsy, cardiomy-opathy, etc. This area of research is indeed exciting and increasingly important, and advances will continue to be made each year. In fact, recent research has shown that there is an equivalent

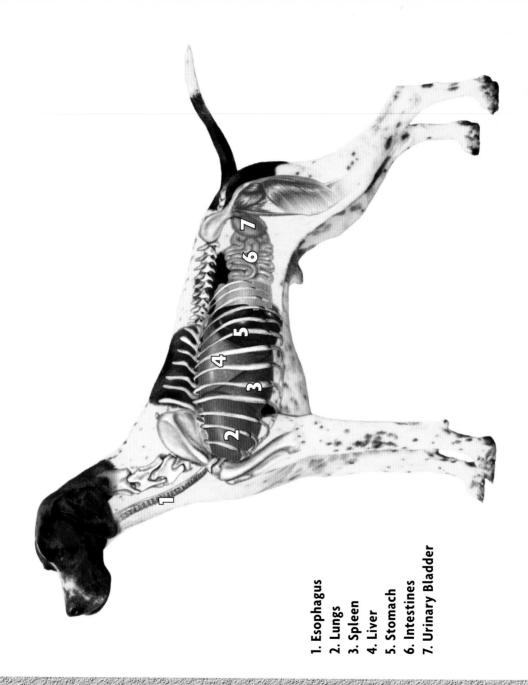

1. Esophagus
2. Lungs
3. Spleen
4. Liver
5. Stomach
6. Intestines
7. Urinary Bladder

Internal Organs of the Pointer

dog gene for 75% of known human genes, so research done in either species is likely to benefit the other.

We've also discussed that evaluating the behavioral nature of your Pointer and that of his immediate family members is an important part of the selection process that cannot be underestimated or overemphasized. It is sometimes difficult to evaluate temperament in puppies because certain behavioral tendencies, such as some forms of aggression, may not be immediately evident. More dogs are euthanized each year for behavioral reasons than for all medical conditions combined, so it is critical to take temperament issues seriously. Start with a well-balanced, friendly companion and put the time and effort into proper socialization, and you will both be rewarded with a lifelong valued relationship.

Assuming that you have started off with a pup from healthy, sound stock, you then become responsible for helping your veterinarian keep your pet healthy. Some crucial things happen before you even bring your puppy home. Parasite control typically begins at two weeks of age, and vaccinations typically begin at six to eight weeks of age. A pre-pubertal evaluation is typically scheduled for about six months of age. At this time, a dental evaluation is done (since the adult teeth are now in), heartworm prevention is started and neutering or spaying is most commonly done.

It is critical to commence regular dental care at home if you have not already done so. It may

DENTAL WARNING SIGNS

A veterinary dental exam is necessary if you notice one or any combination of the following in your dog:
- Broken, loose or missing teeth;
- Loss of appetite (which could be due to mouth pain or illness caused by infection);
- Gum abnormalities, including redness, swelling and bleeding;
- Drooling, with or without blood;
- Yellowing of the teeth or gumline, indicating tartar;
- Bad breath.

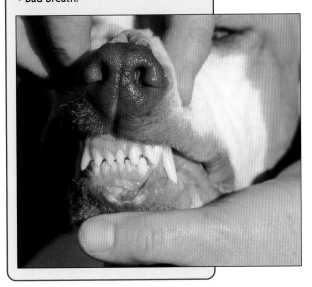

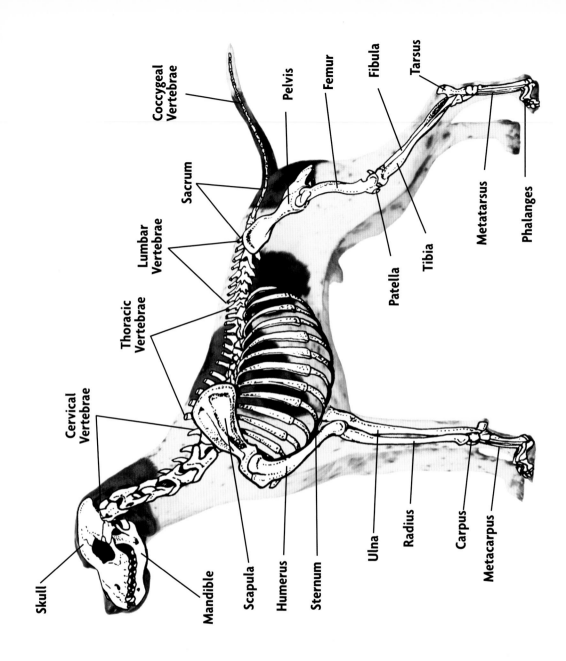

Coccygeal Vertebrae

Pelvis

Femur

Fibula

Tarsus

Sacrum

Lumbar Vertebrae

Thoracic Vertebrae

Cervical Vertebrae

Metatarsus

Phalanges

Patella

Tibia

Skull

Mandible

Scapula

Humerus

Sternum

Ulna

Radius

Carpus

Metacarpus

SKELETAL STRUCTURE OF THE POINTER

not sound very important, but most dogs have active periodontal disease by four years of age if they don't have their teeth cleaned regularly at home, not just at their veterinary exams. Dental problems lead to more than just bad "doggy breath." Gum disease can have very serious medical consequences. If you start brushing your dog's teeth and using antiseptic rinses from a young age, your dog will be accustomed to it and will not resist. The results will be healthy dentition, which your pet will need to enjoy a long, healthy life.

Most dogs are considered adults at a year of age, although some larger breeds still have some filling out to do up to about two or so years old. Even individual dogs within each breed have different healthcare requirements, so work with your veterinarian to determine what will be needed and what your role should be. This doctor-client relationship is important because as vaccination guidelines change, there may not be an annual "vaccine visit" scheduled. You must make sure that you see your veterinarian at least annually even if no vaccines are due because this is the best opportunity to coordinate health-care activities and to make sure that no medical issues creep by unaddressed.

When your Pointer reaches three-quarters of his anticipated lifespan or as the vet recommends, he is considered a "senior" and likely requires some special care. In general, if you've been taking great care of your canine companion throughout his formative and adult years, the transition to senior status should be a smooth one. Age is not a disease, and as long as everything

PROBLEM: AND THAT STARTS WITH "P"

Urinary tract problems more commonly affect female dogs, especially those who have been spayed. The first sign that a urinary tract problem exists usually is a strong odor from the urine or an unusual color. Blood in the urine, known as hematuria, is another sign of an infection, related to cystitis, a bladder infection, bladder cancer or a blood-clotting disorder. Urinary tract problems can also be signaled by the dog's straining while urinating, experiencing pain during urination and genital discharge as well as excessive water intake and urination.

Excessive drinking, in and of itself, does not indicate a urinary tract problem. A dog who is drinking more than normal may have a kidney or liver problem, a hormonal disorder or diabetes mellitus. Behaviorists report a disorder known as psychogenic polydipsia, which manifests itself in excessive drinking and urination. If you notice your dog drinking much more than normal, take him to the vet.

is functioning as it should, there is no reason why most of late adulthood should not be rewarding for both you and your pet. This is especially true if you have tended to the details, such as regular veterinary visits, proper dental care, excellent nutrition and management of bone and joint issues.

At this stage in your Pointer's life, your veterinarian may want to schedule visits twice yearly, instead of once, to run some laboratory screenings, electrocardiograms and the like, and to change the diet to something more digestible. Catching problems early is the best way to manage them effectively. Treating the early stages of heart disease is so much easier than trying to intervene when there is more significant damage to the heart muscle. Similarly, managing the beginning of kidney problems is fairly routine if there is no significant kidney damage. Other problems, like cognitive dysfunction (similar to senility and Alzheimer's disease), cancer, diabetes and arthritis, are more common in older dogs, but all can be treated to help the dog live as many happy, comfortable years as possible. Just as in people, medical management is more effective (and less expensive) when you catch things early.

SELECTING A VETERINARIAN
There is probably no more important decision that you will

> ### YOUR POINTER NEEDS TO VISIT THE VET IF:
> - He has ingested a toxin such as antifreeze or a toxic plant; in these cases, administer first aid and call the vet right away;
> - His teeth are discolored, loose or missing or he has sores or other signs of infection or abnormality in the mouth;
> - He has been vomiting, has had diarrhea or has been constipated for over 24 hours; call immediately if you notice blood;
> - He has refused food for over 24 hours;
> - His eating habits, water intake or toilet habits have noticeably changed; if you have noticed weight gain or weight loss;
> - He shows symptoms of bloat, which requires *immediate* attention;
> - He is salivating excessively;
> - He has a lump in his throat;
> - He has a lump or bumps anywhere on the body;
> - He is very lethargic;
> - He appears to be in pain or otherwise has trouble chewing or swallowing;
> - His skin loses elasticity.
>
> The above are just some of the signs that could be indicative of serious problems that need to be caught as early as possible.

make regarding your pet's healthcare than the selection of his doctor. Your pet's veterinarian will be a pediatrician, family-practice physician and gerontologist, depending on the dog's life stage, and will be the individual who makes recommendations regarding issues such as when specialists need to be consulted, when diagnostic testing and/or therapeutic intervention is needed and when you will need to seek outside emergency and critical-care services. Your vet will act as your advocate and liaison throughout these processes.

Everyone has his own idea about what to look for in a vet, an individual who will play a big role in his dog's (and, of course, his own) life for many years to come. For some, it is the compassionate caregiver with whom they hope to develop a professional relationship to span the lives of their dogs and even their future pets. For others, they are seeking a clinician with keen diagnostic and therapeutic insight who can deliver state-of-the-art healthcare. Still others need a veterinary facility that is open evenings and weekends, is in close proximity or provides mobile veterinary services to accommodate their schedules; these people may not mind that their dogs might see different veterinarians on each visit. Just as we have different reasons for selecting our own healthcare professionals (e.g., covered by insurance plan, expert in field, convenient location, etc.),

we should not expect that there is a one-size-fits-all recommendation for selecting a veterinarian and veterinary practice. The best advice is to be honest in your assessment of what you expect from a veterinary practice and to conscientiously research the options in your area. You will quickly appreciate that not all veterinary practices are the same, and you will be happiest with one that truly meets your needs.

There is another point to be considered in the selection of veterinary services. Not that long ago, a single veterinarian would attempt to manage all medical and surgical issues as they arose. That was often problematic, because veterinarians are trained in many species and many diseases, and it was just

Although your veterinarian will recommend which vaccines are necessary for your Pointer, it's important for you to understand each inoculation and its purpose.

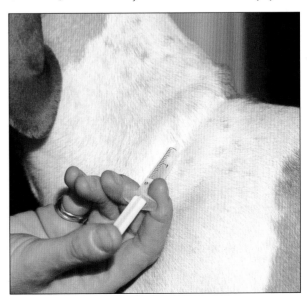

impossible for general veterinary practitioners to be experts in every species, every breed, every field and every ailment. However, just as in the human healthcare fields, specialization has allowed general practitioners to concentrate on primary healthcare delivery, especially wellness and the prevention of infectious diseases, and to utilize a network of specialists to assist in the management of conditions that require specific expertise and experience. Thus there are now many types of veterinary specialists, including dermatologists, cardiologists, ophthalmologists, surgeons, internists, oncologists, neurologists, behaviorists, criticalists and others to help primary-care veterinarians deal with complicated medical challenges. In most cases, specialists see cases referred by primary-care veterinarians, make diagnoses and set up management plans. From there, the animals' ongoing care is returned to their primary-care veterinarians. This important team approach to your pet's medical-care needs has provided opportunities for advanced care and an unparalleled level of quality to be delivered.

With all of the opportunities for your Pointer to receive high-quality veterinary medical care, there is another topic that needs to be addressed at the same time—cost. It's been said that you

INSURANCE FOR PETS

Pet insurance policies are very cost-effective (and very inexpensive by human health-insurance standards), but make sure that you buy the policy long before you intend to use it (preferably starting in puppyhood, because coverage will exclude pre-existing conditions) and that you are actually buying an indemnity insurance plan from an insurance company that is regulated by your state or province. Many insurance policy look-alikes are actually discount clubs that are redeemable only at specific locations and for specific services. An indemnity plan covers your pet at almost all veterinary, specialty and emergency practices and is an excellent way to manage your pet's ongoing healthcare needs.

can have excellent healthcare or inexpensive healthcare, but never both; this is as true in veterinary medicine as it is in human medicine. While veterinary costs are a fraction of what the same services cost in the human health-care arena, it is still difficult to deal with unanticipated medical costs, especially since they can easily creep into hundreds or even thousands of dollars if specialists or emergency services become involved. However, there are ways of managing these risks. The easiest is to buy pet health insurance and realize that its

Do You Know about Hip Dysplasia?

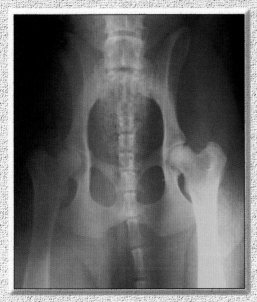

X-ray of a dog with "Good" hips.

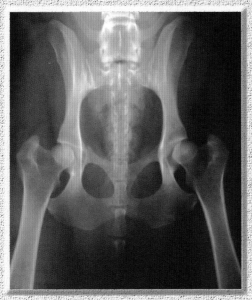

X-ray of a dog with "Moderate" dysplastic hips.

Hip dysplasia is a fairly common condition found in pure-bred dogs. When a dog has hip dysplasia, his hind leg has an incorrectly formed hip joint. By constant use of the hip joint, it becomes more and more loose, wears abnormally and may become arthritic.

Hip dysplasia can only be confirmed with an x-ray, but certain symptoms may indicate a problem. Your dog may have a hip dysplasia problem if he walks in a peculiar manner, hops instead of smoothly runs, uses his hind legs in unison (to keep the pressure off the weak joint), has trouble getting up from a prone position or always sits with both legs together on one side of his body.

As the dog matures, he may adapt well to life with a bad hip, but in a few years the arthritis develops and many dogs with hip dysplasia become crippled.

Hip dysplasia is considered an inherited disease and can be diagnosed definitively by x-ray only when the dog is two years old, although symptoms often appear earlier. Some experts claim that a special diet might help your puppy outgrow the bad hip, but the usual treatments are surgical. The removal of the pectineus muscle, the removal of the round part of the femur, reconstructing the pelvis and replacing the hip with an artificial one are all surgical interventions that are expensive, but they are usually very successful. Follow the advice of your veterinarian.

COMMON INFECTIOUS DISEASES

Let's discuss some of the diseases that create the need for vaccination in the first place. Following are the major canine infectious diseases and a simple explanation of each.

Rabies: A devastating viral disease that can be fatal in dogs and people. In fact, vaccination of dogs and cats is an important public-health measure to create a resistant animal buffer population to protect people from contracting the disease. Vaccination schedules are determined on a government level and are not optional for pet owners; rabies vaccination is required by law in all 50 states.

Parvovirus: A severe, potentially life-threatening disease that is easily transmitted between dogs. There are four strains of the virus, but it is believed that there is significant "cross-protection" between strains that may be included in individual vaccines.

Distemper: A potentially severe and life-threatening disease with a relatively high risk of exposure, especially in certain regions. In very high-risk distemper environments, young pups may be vaccinated with human measles vaccine, a related virus that offers cross-protection when administered at four to ten weeks of age.

Hepatitis: Caused by canine adenovirus type 1 (CAV-1), but since vaccination with the causative virus has a higher rate of adverse effects, cross-protection is derived from the use of adenovirus type 2 (CAV-2), a cause of respiratory disease and one of the potential causes of canine cough. Vaccination with CAV-2 provides long-term immunity against hepatitis, but relatively less protection against respiratory infection.

Canine cough: Also called tracheobronchitis, actually a fairly complicated result of viral and bacterial offenders; therefore, even with vaccination, protection is incomplete. Wherever dogs congregate, canine cough will likely be spread among them. Intranasal vaccination with *Bordetella* and parainfluenza is the best safeguard, but the duration of immunity does not appear to be very long, typically a year at most. These are non-core vaccines, but vaccination is sometimes mandated by boarding kennels, obedience classes, dog shows and other places where dogs congregate to try to minimize spread of infection.

Leptospirosis: A potentially fatal disease that is more common in some geographic regions. It is capable of being spread to humans. The disease varies with the individual "serovar," or strain, of *Leptospira* involved. Since there does not appear to be much cross-protection between serovars, protection is only as good as the likelihood that the serovar in the vaccine is the same as the one in the pet's local environment. Problems with *Leptospira* vaccines are that protection does not last very long, side effects are not uncommon and a large percentage of dogs (perhaps 30%) may not respond to vaccination.

Borrelia burgdorferi: The cause of Lyme disease, the risk of which varies with the geographic area in which the pet lives and travels. Lyme disease is spread by deer ticks in the eastern US and western black-legged ticks in the western part of the country, and the risk of exposure is high in some regions. Lameness, fever and inappetence are most commonly seen in affected dogs. The extent of protection from the vaccine has not been conclusively demonstrated.

Coronavirus: This disease has a high risk of exposure, especially in areas where dogs congregate, but it typically causes only mild to moderate digestive upset (diarrhea, vomiting, etc.). Vaccines are available, but the duration of protection is believed to be relatively short and the effectiveness of the vaccine in preventing infection is considered low.

There are many other vaccinations available, including those for *Giardia* and canine adenovirus-1. While there may be some specific indications for their use, and local risk factors to be considered, they are not widely recommended for most dogs.

foremost purpose is not to cover routine healthcare visits but rather to serve as an umbrella for those rainy days when your pet needs medical care and you don't want to worry about whether or not you can afford that care.

VACCINATIONS AND INFECTIOUS DISEASES

There has never been an easier time to prevent a variety of infectious diseases in your dog, but the advances we've made in veterinary medicine come with a price—choice. Now while it may seem that this choice is a good thing, it also has never been more difficult for the pet owner (or the veterinarian) to make an informed decision about the best way to protect pets through vaccination.

Years ago, it was just accepted that puppies got a starter series of vaccinations and then annual "boosters" throughout their lives to keep them protected. As more and more vaccines became available, consumers wanted the convenience of having all of that protection in a single injection. The result was "multivalent" vaccines that crammed a lot of protection into a single syringe. The manufacturers' recommendations were to give the vaccines annually, and this was a simple enough protocol to follow. However, as veterinary medicine has become more sophisticated and we have started looking more

at healthcare quandaries rather than convenience, it became necessary to reevaluate the situation and deal with some tough questions. It is important to realize that whether or not to use a particular vaccine depends on the risk of contracting the disease against which it protects, the severity of the disease if it is contracted, the duration of immunity provided by the vaccine, the safety of the product and the needs of the individual animal. In a very general sense, rabies, distemper, hepatitis and parvovirus are considered core vaccine needs, while parainfluenza, *Bordetella bronchiseptica*, leptospirosis, coronavirus and borreliosis (Lyme disease) are considered non-core needs and best reserved for animals that demonstrate reasonable risk of contracting the diseases.

NEUTERING/SPAYING

Sterilization procedures (neutering for males/spaying for females) are meant to accomplish several purposes. While the underlying premise is to address the risk of pet overpopulation, there are some medical and behavioral benefits to the surgeries as well. For females, spaying prior to the first estrus (heat cycle) leads to a marked reduction in the risk of mammary cancer and other female health problems. There also will be no

TAKING YOUR DOG'S TEMPERATURE

It is important to know how to take your dog's temperature at times when you think he may be ill. It's not the most enjoyable task, but it can be done without too much difficulty. It's easier with a helper, preferably someone with whom the dog is friendly, so that one of you can hold the dog while the other inserts the thermometer.

Before inserting the thermometer, coat the end with petroleum jelly. Insert the thermometer slowly and gently into the dog's rectum about one inch. Wait for the reading, about two minutes. Be sure to remove the thermometer carefully and clean it thoroughly after each use.

A dog's normal body temperature is between 100.5 and 102.5 degrees F. Immediate veterinary attention is required if the dog's temperature is below 99 or above 104 degrees F.

tion, even no-cost and low-cost neutering options have not eliminated the problem. Perhaps one of the main reasons for this is that individuals that intentionally breed their dogs and those that allow their animals to run at large are the main causes of unwanted offspring. Also, animals in shelters are often there because they were abandoned or relinquished, not because they came from unplanned matings. Neutering/spaying is important, but it should be considered in the context of the real causes of animals' ending up in shelters and eventually being euthanized.

One of the important considerations regarding neutering is that it is a surgical procedure. This sometimes gets lost in discussions of low-cost procedures and commoditization of the process. In females, spaying is specifically referred to as an ovariohysterectomy. In this procedure, a midline incision is made in the abdomen and the entire uterus and both ovaries are surgically removed. While this is a major invasive surgical procedure, it usually has few complications because it is typically performed on healthy, young animals. However, it is major surgery, as any woman who has had a hysterectomy will attest.

In males, neutering has traditionally referred to castration, which involves the surgical

manifestations of "heat" to attract male dogs and no bleeding in the house. For males, there is prevention of testicular cancer and a reduction in the risk of prostate problems. In both sexes there may be some limited reduction in aggressive behaviors toward other dogs and some diminishing of urine marking, roaming and mounting.

While neutering and spaying do indeed prevent animals from contributing to pet overpopula-

Grass seeds, insects and fox-tail barbs are just a few of the irritants found in grass. Check your Pointer's skin and coat often for any sign of abnormality.

removal of both testicles. While still a significant piece of surgery, there is not the abdominal exposure that is required in the female surgery. In addition, there is now a chemical sterilization option in which a solution is injected into each testicle, leading to atrophy of the sperm-producing cells. This can typically be done under sedation rather than full anesthesia. This is a relatively new approach, and there are no long-term clinical studies yet available.

Neutering/spaying is typically done around six months of age at most veterinary hospitals, although techniques have been pioneered to perform the procedures in animals as young as eight weeks of age. In general, the surgeries on the very young animals are done for the specific reason of sterilizing them before they go to their new homes. This is done in some shelter hospitals for assurance that the animals will definitely not produce any pups. Otherwise, these organizations need to rely on owners to comply with their wishes to have the animals "altered" at a later date, something that does not always happen.

There are some exciting immunocontraceptive "vaccines" currently under development, and there may be a time when contraception in pets will not require surgical procedures. We anxiously await these developments.

S. E. M. by Dr. Dennis Kunkel, University of Hawaii

A scanning electron micrograph of a dog flea, *Ctenocephalides canis*, on dog hair.

EXTERNAL PARASITES

FLEAS

Fleas have been around for millions of years and, while we have better tools now for controlling them than at any time in the past, there still is little chance that they will end up on an endangered species list. Actually, they are very well adapted to living on our pets, and they continue to adapt as we make advances.

The female flea can consume 15 times her weight in blood during active reproduction and can lay as many as 40 eggs a day. These eggs are very resistant to the effects of insecticides. They hatch into larvae, which then mature and spin cocoons. The immature fleas reside in this pupal stage until the time is right for feeding. This pupal stage is also very resistant to the effects of insecticides, and pupae can last in the environment without feeding for many months. Newly emergent fleas are attracted to animals by the warmth of the animals' bodies, movement and exhaled carbon dioxide. However, when they first emerge from their cocoons, they orient towards light; thus when an animal passes between a flea and the light source, casting a shadow, the flea pounces and starts to feed. If the animal turns out to be a dog or cat, the reproductive cycle continues. If the flea lands on another type of animal, including a person, the flea will bite but will then look for a more appropriate host. An emerging adult flea can survive without feeding for up to 12 months but, once it tastes blood, it can survive off its host for only 3 to 4 days.

It was once thought that fleas spend most of their lives in the environment, but we now know that fleas won't willingly jump off a dog unless leaping to another dog or when physically removed by brushing, bathing or other manipulation. Flea eggs, on the other hand, are shiny and smooth, and they roll off the animal and into the environment. The eggs, larvae and pupae then exist in the environment, but once the adult finds a susceptible animal, it's home sweet home until the flea is forced to seek refuge elsewhere.

Since adult fleas live on the animal and immature forms survive in the environment, a successful treatment plan must address all stages of the flea life cycle. There are now several safe and effective flea-control products that can be applied on a monthly

FLEA PREVENTION FOR YOUR DOG

- Discuss with your veterinarian the safest product to protect your dog, likely in the form of a monthly tablet or a liquid preparation placed on the back of the dog's neck.
- For dogs suffering from flea-bite dermatitis, a shampoo or topical insecticide treatment is required.
- Your lawn and property should be sprayed with an insecticide designed to kill fleas and ticks that lurk outdoors.
- Using a flea comb, check the dog's coat regularly for any signs of parasites.
- Practice good housekeeping. Vacuum floors, carpets and furniture regularly, especially in the areas that the dog frequents, and wash the dog's bedding weekly.
- Follow up house-cleaning with carpet shampoos and sprays to rid the house of fleas at all stages of development. Insect growth regulators are the safest option.

basis. These include fipronil, imidacloprid, selamectin and permethrin (found in several formulations). Most of these products have significant flea-killing rates within 24 hours. However, none of them will control the immature forms in the environment. To accomplish this, there are a variety of insect growth regulators that can be

THE FLEA'S LIFE CYCLE

What came first, the flea or the egg? This age-old mystery is more difficult to comprehend than the actual cycle of the flea. Fleas usually live only about four months. A female can lay 2,000 eggs in her lifetime.

Egg

After ten days of rolling around your carpet or under your furniture, the eggs hatch into larvae, which feed on various and sundry debris.

Larva

In days or months, depending on the climate, the larvae spin cocoons and develop into the pupal or nymph stage, which quickly develop into fleas.

Pupa

These immature fleas must locate a host within 10 to 14 days or they will die. Only about 1% of the flea population exist as adult fleas, while the other 99% exist as eggs, larvae or pupae.

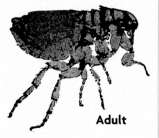

Adult

Photo by Carolina Biological Supply Co.

Photo by Carolina Biological Supply Co.

KILL FLEAS THE NATURAL WAY

If you choose not to go the route of conventional medication, there are some natural ways to ward off fleas:

- Dust your dog with a natural flea powder, composed of such herbal goodies as rosemary, wormwood, pennyroyal, citronella, rue, tobacco powder and eucalyptus.
- Apply diatomaceous earth, the fossilized remains of single-cell algae, to your carpets, furniture and pet's bedding. Even though it's not good for dogs, it's even worse for fleas, which will dry up swiftly and die.
- Brush your dog frequently, give him adequate exercise and let him fast occasionally. All of these activities strengthen the dog's immune system and make him more resistant to disease and parasites.
- Bathe your dog with a capful of pennyroyal or eucalyptus oil.
- Feed a natural diet, free of additives and preservatives. Add a little fresh garlic and brewer's yeast to the dog's morning portion, as these items have flea-repelling properties.

sprayed into the environment (e.g., pyriproxyfen, methoprene, fenoxycarb) as well as insect development inhibitors such as lufenuron that can be administered. These compounds have no effect on adult fleas, but they stop immature forms from developing into adults. In years gone by, we relied heavily on toxic insecticides (such as organophosphates, organochlorines and carbamates) to manage the flea problem, but today's options are not only much safer to use on our pets but also safer for the environment.

TICKS

Ticks are members of the spider class (arachnids) and are blood-sucking parasites capable of transmitting a variety of diseases, including Lyme disease, ehrlichiosis, babesiosis and Rocky Mountain spotted fever. It's easy to see ticks on your own skin, but it is more of a challenge when your furry companion is affected. Whenever you happen to be planning a stroll in a tick-infested area (especially forests, grassy or wooded areas or parks) be prepared to do a thorough inspection of your dog afterward to search for ticks. Ticks can be tricky, so make sure you spend time looking in the ears, between the toes and everywhere else where a tick might hide. Ticks need to be attached for 24–72 hours before they transmit most of the diseases that they carry, so you do have a window of opportunity for some preventive intervention.

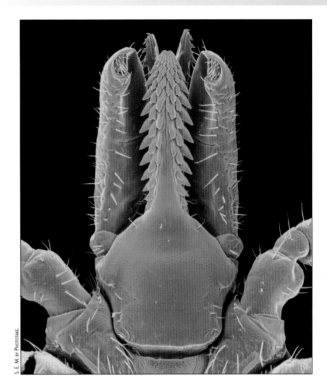

S. E. M. BY PHOTOTAKE.

A TICKING BOMB

There is nothing good about a tick's harpooning his nose into your dog's skin. Among the diseases caused by ticks are Rocky Mountain spotted fever, canine ehrlichiosis, canine babesiosis, canine hepatozoonosis and Lyme disease. If a dog is allergic to the saliva of a female wood tick, he can develop tick paralysis.

Female ticks live to eat and breed. They can lay between 4,000 and 5,000 eggs and they die soon after. Males, on the other hand, live only to mate with the females and continue the process as long as they are able. Most ticks live on multiple hosts before parasitizing dogs. The immature forms typically reside on grass and shrubs, waiting for susceptible animals to walk by. The larvae and nymph stages typically feed on wildlife.

If only a few ticks are present on a dog, they can be plucked out, but it is important to remove the entire head and mouthparts,

A scanning electron micrograph of the head of a female deer tick, *Ixodes dammini*, a parasitic tick that carries Lyme disease.

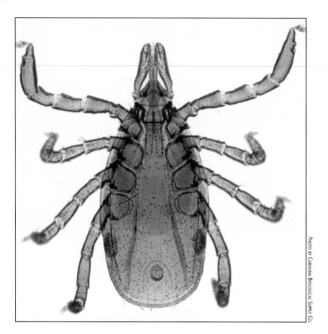

Deer tick,
Ixodes dammini.

disposed of in a container of alcohol or household bleach.

Some of the newer flea products, specifically those with fipronil, selamectin and permethrin, have effect against some, but not all, species of tick. Flea collars containing appropriate pesticides (e.g., propoxur, chlorfenvinphos) can aid in tick control. In most areas, such collars should be placed on animals in March, at the beginning of the tick season, and changed regularly. Leaving the collar on when the pesticide level is waning invites the development of resistance. Amitraz collars are also good for tick control, and the active ingredient does not interfere with other flea-control products. The ingredient helps prevent the attachment of ticks to the skin and will cause those ticks already on the skin to detach themselves.

which may be deeply embedded in the skin. This is best accomplished with forceps designed especially for this purpose; fingers can be used but should be protected with rubber gloves, plastic wrap or at least a paper towel. The tick should be grasped as closely as possible to the animal's skin and should be pulled upward with steady, even pressure. Do not squeeze, crush or puncture the body of the tick or you risk exposure to any disease carried by that tick. Once the ticks have been removed, the sites of attachment should be disinfected. Your hands should then be washed with soap and water to further minimize risk of contagion. The tick should be

TICK CONTROL

Removal of underbrush and leaf litter and the thinning of trees in areas where tick control is desired are recommended. These actions remove the cover and food sources for small animals that serve as hosts for ticks. With continued mowing of grasses in these areas, the probability of ticks' surviving is further reduced. A variety of insecticide ingredients (e.g., resmethrin, carbaryl, permethrin, chlorpyrifos, dioxathion and allethrin) are registered for tick control around the home.

PHOTO BY CAROLINA BIOLOGICAL SUPPLY CO.

MITES

Mites are tiny arachnid parasites that parasitize the skin of dogs. Skin diseases caused by mites are referred to as "mange," and there are many different forms seen in dogs. These forms are very different from one another, each one warranting an individual description.

Sarcoptic mange, or scabies, is one of the itchiest conditions that affects dogs. The microscopic *Sarcoptes* mites burrow into the superficial layers of the skin and can drive dogs crazy with itchiness. They are also communicable to people, although they can't complete their reproductive cycle on people. In addition to being tiny, the mites also are often difficult to find when trying to make a diagnosis. Skin scrapings from multiple areas are examined microscopically but, even then, sometimes the mites cannot be found.

Fortunately, scabies is relatively easy to treat, and there are a variety of products that will successfully kill the mites. Since the mites can't live in the environment for very long without feeding, a complete cure is usually possible within four to eight weeks.

Cheyletiellosis is caused by a relatively large mite, which sometimes can be seen even without a microscope. Often referred to as "walking dandruff," this also causes itching, but not usually as profound as with scabies.

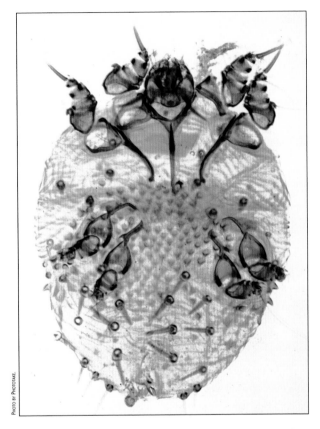

PHOTO BY PHOTOTAKE.

Sarcoptes scabiei, commonly known as the "itch mite."

While *Cheyletiella* mites can survive somewhat longer in the environment than scabies mites, they too are relatively easy to treat, being responsive to not only the medications used to treat scabies but also often to flea-control products.

Otodectes cynotis is the canine ear mite and is one of the more common causes of mange, especially in young dogs in shelters or pet stores. That's because the mites are typically present in large numbers and are quickly spread to

Micrograph of a dog louse, *Heterodoxus spiniger*. Female lice attach their eggs to the hairs of the dog. As the eggs hatch, the larval lice bite and feed on the blood. Lice can also feed on dead skin and hair. This feeding activity can cause hair loss and skin problems.

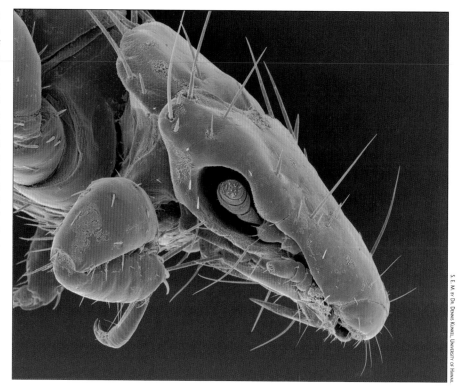

S. E. M. by Dr. Dennis Kunkel, University of Hawaii

nearby animals. The mites rarely do much harm but can be difficult to eradicate if the treatment regimen is not comprehensive. While many try to treat the condition with ear drops only, this is the most common cause of treatment failure. Ear drops cause the mites to simply move out of the ears and as far away as possible (usually to the base of the tail) until the insecticide levels in the ears drop to an acceptable level—then it's back to business as usual! The successful treatment of ear mites requires treating all animals in the household with a systemic insecticide, such as selamectin, or a combination of miticidal ear drops combined with whole-body flea-control preparations.

Demodicosis, sometimes referred to as red mange, can be one of the most difficult forms of mange to treat. Part of the problem has to do with the fact that the mites live in the hair follicles and they are relatively well shielded from topical and systemic products. The main issue, however, is that demodectic mange typically results only when there is some underlying process interfering with the dog's immune system.

Since *Demodex* mites are

normal residents of the skin of mammals, including humans, there is usually a mite population explosion only when the immune system fails to keep the number of mites in check. In young animals, the immune deficit may be transient or may reflect an actual inherited immune problem. In older animals, demodicosis is usually seen only when there is another disease hampering the immune system, such as diabetes, cancer, thyroid problems or the use of immune-suppressing drugs. Accordingly, treatment involves not only trying to kill the mange mites but also discerning what is interfering with immune function and correcting it if possible.

Chiggers represent several different species of mite that don't parasitize dogs specifically, but do latch on to passersby and can cause irritation. The problem is most prevalent in wooded areas in the late summer and fall. Treatment is not difficult, as the mites do not complete their life cycle on dogs and are susceptible to a variety of miticidal products.

MOSQUITOES

Mosquitoes have long been known to transmit a variety of diseases to people, as well as just being biting pests during warm weather. They also pose a real risk to pets. Not only do they carry deadly heartworms but recently there also has been much concern over their involvement with West Nile virus. While we can avoid heartworm with the use of preventive medications, there are no such preventives for West Nile virus. The only method of prevention in endemic areas is active mosquito control. Fortunately, most dogs that have been exposed to the virus only developed flu-like symptoms and, to date, there have not been the large number of reported deaths in canines as seen in some other species.

ILLUSTRATION BY PHOTOTAKE

Illustration of Demodex folliculoram.

MOSQUITO REPELLENT

Low concentrations of DEET (less than 10%), found in many human mosquito repellents, have been safely used in dogs but, in these concentrations, probably give only about two hours of protection. DEET may be safe in these small concentrations, but since it is not licensed for use on dogs, there is no research proving its safety for dogs. Products containing permethrin give the longest-lasting protection, perhaps two to four weeks. As DEET is not licensed for use on dogs, and both DEET and permethrin can be quite toxic to cats, appropriate care should be exercised. Other products, such as those containing oil of citronella, also have some mosquito-repellent activity, but typically have a relatively short duration of action.

The ascarid roundworm *Toxocara canis*, showing the mouth with three lips. INSET: Photomicrograph of the roundworm *Ascaris lumbricoides*.

ASCARID DANGERS

The most commonly encountered worms in dogs are roundworms known as ascarids. *Toxascaris leonine* and *Toxocara canis* are the two species that infect dogs. Subsisting in the dog's stomach and intestines, adult roundworms can grow to 7 inches in length and adult females can lay in excess of 200,000 eggs in a single day.

In humans, visceral larval migrans affects people who have ingested eggs of *Toxocara canis*, which frequently contaminates children's sandboxes, beaches and park grounds. The roundworms reside in the human's stomach and intestines, as they would in a dog's, but do not mature. Instead, they find their way to the liver, lungs and skin, or even to the heart or kidneys in severe cases. Deworming puppies is critical in preventing the infection in humans, and young children should never handle nursing pups who have not been dewormed.

INTERNAL PARASITES: WORMS

ASCARIDS

Ascarids are intestinal roundworms that rarely cause severe disease in dogs. Nonetheless, they are of major public health significance because they can be transferred to people. Sadly, it is children who are most commonly affected by the parasite, probably from inadvertently ingesting ascarid-contaminated soil. In fact, many yards and children's sandboxes contain appreciable numbers of ascarid eggs. So, while ascarids don't bite dogs or latch onto their intestines to suck blood, they do cause some nasty medical conditions in children and are best eradicated from our furry friends. Because pups can start passing ascarid eggs by three weeks of age, most parasite-control programs begin at two weeks of age and are repeated every two weeks until pups are eight weeks old. It is important to

HOOKED ON ANCYLOSTOMA

Adult dogs can become infected by the bloodsucking nematodes we commonly call hookworms via ingesting larvae from the ground or via the larvae penetrating the dog's skin. It is not uncommon for infected dogs to show no symptoms of hookworm infestation. Sometimes symptoms occur within ten days of exposure. These symptoms can include bloody diarrhea, anemia, loss of weight and general weakness. Dogs pass the hookworm eggs in their stools, which serves as the vet's method of identifying the infestation. The hookworm larvae can encyst themselves in the dog's tissues and be released when the dog is experiencing stress.

Caused by an *Ancylostoma* species whose common host is the dog, cutaneous larval migrans affects humans, causing itching and lumps and streaks beneath the surface of the skin.

realize that bitches can pass ascarids to their pups even if they test negative prior to whelping. Accordingly, bitches are best treated at the same time as the pups.

HOOKWORMS

Unlike ascarids, hookworms do latch onto a dog's intestinal tract and can cause significant loss of blood and protein. Similar to ascarids, hookworms can be transmitted to humans, where they cause a condition known as cutaneous larval migrans. Dogs can become infected either by consuming the infective larvae or by the larvae's penetrating the skin directly. People most often get infected when they are lying on the ground (such as on a beach) and the larvae penetrate the skin. Yes, the larvae can penetrate through a beach blanket. Hookworms are typically susceptible to the same medications used to treat ascarids.

The hookworm *Ancylostoma caninum* infests the intestines of dogs. INSET: Note the row of hooks at the posterior end, used to anchor the worm to the intestinal wall.

WHIPWORMS

Whipworms latch onto the lower aspects of the dog's colon and can cause cramping and diarrhea. Eggs do not start to appear in the dog's feces until about three months after the dog was infected. This worm has a peculiar life cycle, which makes it more difficult to control than ascarids or hookworms. The good thing is that whipworms rarely are transferred to people.

Some of the medications used to treat ascarids and hookworms are also effective against whipworms, but, in general, a separate treatment protocol is needed. Since most of the medications are effective against the adults but not the eggs or larvae, treatment is typically repeated in three weeks, and then often in three

WORM-CONTROL GUIDELINES
- Practice sanitary habits with your dog and home.
- Clean up after your dog and don't let him sniff or eat other dogs' droppings.
- Control insects and fleas in the dog's environment. Fleas, lice, cockroaches, beetles, mice and rats can act as hosts for various worms.
- Prevent dogs from eating uncooked meat, raw poultry and dead animals.
- Keep dogs and children from playing in sand and soil.
- Kennel dogs on cement or gravel; avoid dirt runs.
- Administer heartworm preventives regularly.
- Have your vet examine your dog's stools at your annual visits.
- Select a boarding kennel carefully so as to avoid contamination from other dogs or an unsanitary environment.
- Prevent dogs from roaming. Obey local leash laws.

Adult whipworm, *Trichuris* sp., an intestinal parasite.

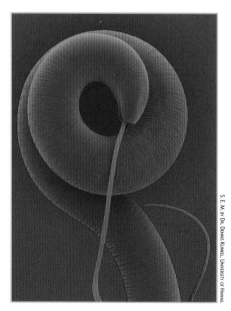

S. E. M. BY DR. DENNIS KUNKEL, UNIVERSITY OF HAWAII.

months as well. Unfortunately, since dogs don't develop resistance to whipworms, it is difficult to prevent them from getting reinfected if they visit soil contaminated with whipworm eggs.

TAPEWORMS

There are many different species of tapeworm that affect dogs, but *Dipylidium caninum* is probably the most common and is spread by fleas. Flea larvae feed on organic debris and tapeworm eggs in the environment, and when a dog chews at himself and manages to ingest fleas, he might get a dose of tapeworm at the same time. The tapeworm then develops further in the intestine of the dog.

The tapeworm itself, which is a parasitic flatworm that latches onto the intestinal wall, is composed of numerous segments. When the segments break off into the intestine (as proglottids), they may accumulate around the rectum, like grains of rice. While this tapeworm is disgusting in its behavior, it is not directly communicable to humans (although humans can also get infected by swallowing fleas).

A much more dangerous flatworm is *Echinococcus multilocularis*, which is typically found in foxes, coyotes and wolves. The eggs are passed in the feces and infect rodents, and when dogs eat the rodents, the dogs can be infected by thousands of adult tapeworms. While the parasites don't cause many problems in dogs, this is considered the most lethal worm infection that people can get. Take appropriate precautions if you live in an area in which these tapeworms are found. Do not use mulch that may contain feces of dogs, cats or wildlife, and

discourage your pets from hunting wildlife. Treat these tapeworm infections aggressively in pets because if humans get infected, approximately half die.

HEARTWORMS

Heartworm disease is caused by the parasite *Dirofilaria immitis* and is seen in dogs around the world. A member of the roundworm group, it is spread between dogs by the bite of an infected mosquito. The mosquito injects infective larvae into the dog's skin with its bite, and these larvae develop under the skin for a period of time before making their way to the heart. There they develop into adults, which grow and create blockages of the heart, lungs and major blood vessels there. They also start producing offspring (microfilariae),

A dog tapeworm proglottid (body segment).

The dog tapeworm *Taenia pisiformis*.

A Look at Internal Parasites

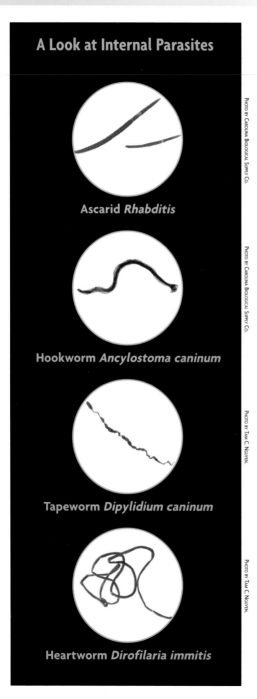

Ascarid *Rhabditis*

Hookworm *Ancylostoma caninum*

Tapeworm *Dipylidium caninum*

Heartworm *Dirofilaria immitis*

PHOTO BY CAROLINA BIOLOGICAL SUPPLY CO.

PHOTO BY CAROLINA BIOLOGICAL SUPPLY CO.

PHOTO BY TAM C. NGUYEN

PHOTO BY TAM C. NGUYEN

and these microfilariae circulate in the bloodstream, waiting to hitch a ride when the next mosquito bites. Once in the mosquito, the microfilariae develop into infective larvae and the entire process is repeated.

When dogs get infected with heartworm, over time they tend to develop symptoms associated with heart disease, such as coughing, exercise intolerance and potentially many other manifestations. Diagnosis is confirmed by either seeing the microfilariae themselves in blood samples or using immunologic tests (antigen testing) to identify the presence of adult heartworms. Since antigen tests measure the presence of adult heartworms and microfilarial tests measure offspring produced by adults, neither are positive until six to seven months after the initial infection. However, the beginning of damage can occur by fifth-stage larvae as early as three months after infection. Thus it is possible for dogs to be harboring problem-causing larvae for up to three months before either type of test would identify an infection.

The good news is that there are great protocols available for preventing heartworm in dogs. Testing is critical in the process, and it is important to understand the benefits as well as the limitations of such testing. All dogs six months of age or older that have not been on continuous heartworm-preventive medication should be

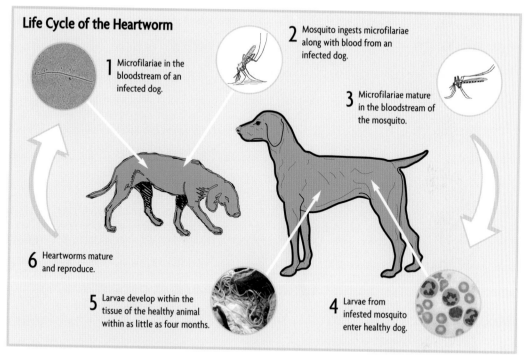

Life Cycle of the Heartworm

1 Microfilariae in the bloodstream of an infected dog.

2 Mosquito ingests microfilariae along with blood from an infected dog.

3 Microfilariae mature in the bloodstream of the mosquito.

4 Larvae from infested mosquito enter healthy dog.

5 Larvae develop within the tissue of the healthy animal within as little as four months.

6 Heartworms mature and reproduce.

screened with microfilarial or antigen tests. For dogs receiving preventive medication, periodic antigen testing helps assess the effectiveness of the preventives. The American Heartworm Society guidelines suggest that annual retesting may not be necessary when owners have absolutely provided continuous heartworm prevention. Retesting on a two- to three-year interval may be sufficient in these cases. However, your veterinarian will likely have specific guidelines under which heartworm preventives will be prescribed, and many prefer to err on the side of safety and retest annually.

It is indeed fortunate that heartworm is relatively easy to prevent because treatments can be as life-threatening as the disease itself. Treatment requires a two-step process that kills the adult heartworms first and then the microfilariae. Prevention is obviously preferable; this involves a once-monthly oral or topical treatment. The most common oral preventives include ivermectin (not suitable for some breeds), moxidectin and milbemycin oxime; the once-a-month topical drug selamectin provides heartworm protection in addition to flea, some types of tick and other parasite controls.

POINTER

Who can deny that the multi-talented Pointer is also a handsome dog? Certainly the founders of the famous Westminster Kennel Club thought so, as they selected the silhouette of the breed as the club's logo. Even if your Pointer is only a pet, this chapter will give you much useful information about the American Kennel Club and the United Kennel Club, the two largest all-breed clubs in the US, and the conformation shows and trials that they sponsor. Perhaps you would like to take a try at showing your Pointer in a dog show or an obedience trial. Many pet owners pursue the Canine Good Citizen® Program with their well-behaved companions. Depending on where your dog is registered, that is the club you would investigate. If yours is a weekend hunting dog, you might consider a hunting test or even a field trial.

Many pet owners enter their "average" Pointers in dog shows for the fun and enjoyment of it. Dog showing makes an absorbing hobby, with many rewards for dogs and owners alike. If you're having fun, meeting other people who share your interests and enjoying the overall experience, you likely will catch the "bug."

AKC DOG SHOWS
Visiting a dog show as a spectator is a great place to start. Pick up the show catalog to find out what time your breed is being shown, who is judging the breed and in which ring the classes will be held. To start, Pointers compete

---

FOR MORE INFORMATION...
For reliable up-to-date information about registration, dog shows and other canine competitions, contact one of the national registries by mail or via the Internet.

American Kennel Club
5580 Centerview Dr., Raleigh, NC 27606-3390
www.akc.org

United Kennel Club
100 E. Kilgore Road, Kalamazoo, MI 49002
www.ukcdogs.com

Canadian Kennel Club
89 Skyway Ave., Suite 100, Etobicoke, Ontario
M9W 6R4, Canada
www.ckc.ca

The Kennel Club
1-5 Clarges St., Piccadilly, London W1Y 8AB, UK
www.the-kennel-club.org.uk

against other Pointers, and the winner is selected as Best of Breed by the judge. This is the procedure for each breed. At a group show, all of the Best of Breed winners go on to compete for Group One in their respective groups. For example, all Best of Breed winners in a given group compete against each other; this is done for all seven groups. Finally, all seven group winners go head to head in the ring for the Best in Show award.

What most spectators don't understand is the basic idea of conformation. A dog show is often referred as a "conformation" show. This means that the judge should decide how each dog stacks up (conforms) to the breed standard for his given breed: how well does this Pointer conform to the ideal representative detailed in the standard? Ideally, this is what happens. In reality, however, this ideal often gets slighted as the judge compares Pointer #1 to Pointer #2. Again, the ideal is that each dog is judged based on his merits in comparison to his breed standard, not in comparison to the other dogs in the ring. It is easier for judges to compare dogs of the same breed to decide which they think is the better specimen; in the Group and Best in Show ring, however, it is very difficult to compare one breed to another, like apples to oranges. Thus the dog's conformation to the breed

The Pointer continues to thrive on both sides of the Atlantic. British show dogs have complemented American lines for generations.

standard is essential to success in conformation shows. The dog described in the standard is the perfect dog of that breed, and breeders keep their eye on the standard when they choose which dogs to breed, hoping to get closer and closer to the ideal with each litter.

Three kinds of conformation shows are offered by the AKC. There is the all-breed show, in which all AKC-recognized breeds can compete; the specialty show, which is for one breed only and usually sponsored by the breed's parent club; and the group show, for all breeds in one of the AKC's seven groups. The Pointer competes in the Sporting Group.

For a dog to become an AKC champion of record, the dog must earn 15 points at shows. The points must be awarded by at least three different judges and must include two "majors" under different judges. A "major" is a three-, four- or five-point win, and the number of points per win is determined by the number of dogs competing in the show on that day. (Dogs that are absent or are excused are not counted.) The number of points that are awarded varies from breed to breed. More dogs are needed to attain a major in more popular breeds, and fewer dogs are needed in less popular breeds. Yearly, the AKC evaluates the number of dogs in competition in each division (there are 14 divisions in all, based on geography) and may or may not change the numbers of dogs required for each number of points.

Whether it's your first show or your hundredth, dress like a professional and act the part.

Only one dog and one bitch of each breed can win points at a given show. Dogs and bitches do not compete against each other until they are champions. Dogs that are not champions (referred to as "class dogs") compete in one of five classes. The class in which a dog is entered depends on age and previous show wins. First there is the Puppy Class (sometimes divided further into classes for 6- to 9-month-olds and 9- to 12-month-olds); next is the Novice Class (for dogs that have no points toward their championship and whose only first-place wins have come in the Puppy Class or the Novice Class, the latter class limited to three first places); then there is the American-bred Class (for dogs bred in the US); the Bred-by-Exhibitor Class (for dogs handled by their breeders or by immediate family members of their breeders) and the Open Class (for any non-champions). Any dog may enter the Open Class, regardless of age or win history, but to be competitive the dog should be older and have ring experience.

The judge at the show begins judging the male dogs in the Puppy Class(es) and proceeds through the other classes. The judge awards first through fourth place in each class. The first-place winners of each class then compete with one another in the Winners Class to determine

BECOMING AN AKC CHAMPION

An official AKC championship of record requires that a dog accumulate 15 points under three different judges, including two "majors" under different judges. Points are awarded based on the number of dogs entered into competition, varying from breed to breed and place to place. A win of three, four or five points is considered a "major." The AKC annually assigns a schedule of points to adjust for variations that accompany a breed's popularity and the population of a given area.

Winners Dog. The judge then starts over with the bitches, beginning with the Puppy Class(es) and proceeding up to the Winners Class to award Winners Bitch, just as he did with the dogs. A Reserve Winners Dog and Reserve Winners Bitch are also selected; they could be awarded the points in the case of a disqualification.

The Winners Dog and Winners Bitch are the two that are awarded the points for their breed. They then go on to compete with any champions of record (often called "specials") of their breed that are entered in the show. The champions may be dogs or bitches; in this class, all are shown together. The judge reviews the Winners Dog and Winners Bitch along with all of the champions to select the Best of Breed winner. The Best of Winners is selected between the Winners Dog and Winners Bitch; if one of these two is selected Best of Breed as well, he or she is automatically determined Best of Winners. Lastly, the judge selects Best of Opposite Sex to the Best of Breed winner. The Best of Breed winner then goes on to the group competition.

At a group or all-breed show, the Best of Breed winners from each breed are divided into their respective groups to compete against one another for Group One through Group Four. Group One (first place) is awarded to the dog that best lives up to the ideal for his breed as described in the standard. A group judge, therefore, must have a thorough working knowledge of many breed standards. After placements have been made in each group, the

Ch. Luftnase Albelarm Bee's Knees, shown by Michael Zollo to BIS at Westchester KC in 1989. She was top Sporting Dog and #2 of all breeds that year as well, winning over 40 BIS.

A first-place Pointer strikes a winning pose with his handler.

seven Group One winners (from the Sporting Group, Toy Group, Hound Group, etc.) compete against each other for the top honor, Best in Show.

UKC DOG SHOWS

UKC dog shows may be held for one breed only, several breeds or all breeds. UKC shows are arranged differently from the conformation shows of other organizations. Entries are restricted by age, and you cannot show your dog in a class other than his correct age class. When you compete for championship points, you may enter Puppy (6–12 months), Junior (1–2 years), Senior (2–3 years) or Adult (3 years and older). You may also enter the Breeder/Handler Class, where dogs of all ages compete,

but the dog must be handled by his breeder or a member of the breeder's immediate family. The winners of each class compete for Best Male or Best Female. These two dogs then compete for Best of Winners; the dog who is given this award will go on to compete for Best of Breed. Best of Breed competition includes the Best of Winners and dogs that have earned Champion and Grand Champion titles. Earning Best Male or Best Female, as long as there is competition, is considered a "major."

Once a dog has earned three "majors" and accumulated 100 points, he is considered a UKC champion. What this means is that the dog is now ready to compete for the title of Grand Champion, which is equivalent to an AKC championship. To earn the Grand Champion title, a dog must compete with a minimum of two other dogs who are also champions. The dog must win this class, called the Champion of Champions class, five times under three different judges. In rare breeds, it is difficult to assemble a class of champions, so the UKC Grand Champion title is truly a prestigious one. Once a dog has earned the Grand Champion title, he can continue to compete for Top Ten, but there are no further titles to earn. "Top Ten" refers to the ten dogs in each breed that have won the most points in a

CLASSES AT UNITED KENNEL CLUB DOG SHOWS

The Regular classes, for all dogs who are not Champions or Grand Champions, are divided by sex (and variety, where applicable) with four winners selected by the judge. Champions and Grand Champions are judged separately, with one winner in each class. The Regular classes are broken down into the following:

Puppy Class: Male and female puppies, from six months to one year of age.

Junior Class: Male and female dogs, from one year to under two years of age.

Senior Class: Male and female dogs, from two years of age to under three years of age.

Adult Class: Male and female dogs, three years of age and older.

Breeder/Handler Class: Male and female dogs, six months of age and older, handled by the breeder of record or a member of the breeder's immediate family.

given year. These dogs compete in a Top Ten invitational competition annually.

The breeds recognized by the UKC are divided into groups. The Pointer competes in the Gun Dog Group, which consists of dogs of similar utility and/or heritage. Depending on the show-giving club, group competition may or may not be offered. A group must have a minimum of five breeds entered in order for group competition to take place. If group competition is offered, Best in Show competition consists of the group winners. If there is no group competition, then all Best of Breed dogs go into the ring at the same time to compete for Best in Show. This can be a large number of dogs and thus can be very interesting, to say the least!

Aside from the variations already presented, UKC shows differ from other dog shows in one very significant way: no professional handlers are allowed to show dogs, except for those dogs they own themselves. UKC shows create an atmosphere that is owner-friendly, relaxed and genuinely fun. Bait in the ring is allowed at the discretion of the judge, but throwing the bait, dropping it on the floor or other "handler tricks" will get an owner excused from the ring in a big hurry.

In addition to dog shows, the UKC offers many, many more venues for dogs and their owners, in keeping with its mission of promoting the "total dog." UKC obedience events test the training of dogs as they perform a series of prescribed exercises at the commands of their handlers. There are several levels of competition, ranging from basic commands such as "sit," "come" and "heel," to advanced exercises like scent discrimination and directed retrieves over jumps, based on the dog's level of accomplishment. The classes are further delineated by the experience of the handler.

OBEDIENCE TRIALS

Any dog that is registered, regardless of neutering or other disqualifications that would preclude entry in conformation competition, can participate in obedience trials. There are three levels of difficulty in AKC obedience competition. The first (and easiest) level is the Novice, in which dogs can earn the

Companion Dog (CD) title. The intermediate level is the Open level, in which the Companion Dog Excellent (CDX) title is awarded. The advanced level is the Utility level, in which dogs compete for the Utility Dog (UD) title. Classes at each level are further divided into "A" and "B," with "A" for beginners and "B" for those with more experience. In order to win a title at a given level, a dog must earn three "legs." A "leg" is accomplished when a dog scores 170 or higher (200 is a perfect score). The scoring system gets a little trickier when you understand that a dog must score more than 50% of the points available for each exercise in order to actually earn the points. Available points for each exercise range between 20 and 40.

A dog must complete different exercises at each level of obedience. The Novice exercises are the easiest, with the Open and finally the Utility levels progressing in difficulty. Examples of Novice exercises are on- and off-lead heeling, a figure-8 pattern, performing a recall (or come), long sit, long down and standing for examination. In the Open level, the Novice-level exercises are required again, but this time without a leash and for longer durations. In addition, the dog must clear a broad jump, retrieve over a jump and drop on recall. In the Utility level, the

Ch. Kinnike CP Schofield, JH, CD is a champion shown here finishing his obedience title at ten years of age.

exercises are quite difficult, including executing basic commands based on hand signals, following a complex heeling pattern, locating articles based on scent discrimination and completing jumps at the handler's direction.

Once he's earned the UD title, a dog can go on to win the prestigious title of Utility Dog Excellent (UDX) by winning "legs" in ten shows. Additionally, Utility Dogs who win "legs" in Open B and Utility B earn points toward the lofty title of Obedience Trial Champion (OTCh.).

UKC obedience differs from AKC obedience in many respects. Even at the most basic levels, the dogs are expected to "honor" other dogs who are working. In other words, the "honoring" dog

must be placed in a down/stay while his owner leaves the ring and moves out of sight. The dog must remain in the down/stay position while the working dog goes through the heeling exercises.

AGILITY TRIALS

Agility events are fast-paced exercises in which the handler directs his dog through a course of exercises and obstacles in a race against the clock. The dogs are scored according to the manner in which they negotiate the obstacles and the time elapsed to complete the course. Agility trials became sanctioned by the AKC in August 1994, when the first licensed agility trials were held. The AKC allows all registered breeds to participate, providing the dog is

While the judge reviews the breed line-up, the exhibitors must keep their dogs stacked (standing in show pose) and attentive.

12 months of age or older. Agility is designed so that the handler demonstrates how well the dog can work at his side. The handler directs his dog through, over, under and around an obstacle course that includes jumps, tires, a sway bridge, the dog walk, weave poles, pipe tunnels, collapsed tunnels and more. While working his way through the course, the dog must keep one eye and ear on the handler and the rest of his body on the course. The handler runs along with the dog, giving verbal and hand signals to guide the dog through the course. UKC agility is very similar to AKC agility; clubs often will offer both AKC and UKC agility events (not on the same day).

The first organization to promote agility trials in the US was the United States Dog Agility Association, Inc. (USDAA). Established in 1986, the USDAA sparked the formation of many member clubs around the country. To participate in USDAA trials, dogs must be at least 18 months of age. All three clubs offer titles to winning dogs, although the exercises and requirements of the organizations differ.

Agility trials are a great way to keep your dog active, and they will keep you running, too! You should join a local agility club to learn more about the sport. These clubs offer sessions in which you can introduce your dog to the various obstacles as well as training classes to prepare him for competition. In no time, your dog will be climbing A-frames, crossing the dog walk and flying over hurdles, all with you right beside him. Your heart will leap every time your dog jumps through the hoop—and you'll be having just as much (if not more) fun!

FIELD TRIALS
Field trials are offered to the retrievers, pointers and spaniel breeds of the Sporting Group as well as to the Beagles, Dachshunds and Bassets of the Hound Group. The purpose of field trials is to demonstrate a

EXCELLENCE IN OTHER PURSUITS

While the breed excels naturally in the field and conformation, the areas of obedience, agility and tracking have never been dominated by the Pointer. There are some notable exceptions that we are happy to point out here. The first Pointer to earn the Obedience Trial Champion title was OTCh./Am./Can. Ch. Scanpoint Sunrise Serenade, owner-handled and trained by Lynn Deering and co-owned with Karin Ashe. Sunny won the OTCh. in 1984. Another rare Pointer indeed is OTCh./MACH/U-CD Longtrail Piece of My Heart, UDX, who was the second OTCh. Known as "Champer," he is the first Pointer to earn not only the MACH agility title but also the NAJ, AXJ and MXJ "jumper" agility titles. He is trained by owner Julie Hill. The first UDX titleholder was Ch. Scanpoint's Barefoot Contessa, UDX, owned by Lynn Deering. She won the title in 1995. The first Tracking Dog Excellent title to be won by a Pointer went to Eclipse Final Fling Nthfld, JH, TDX on April 27, 2003.

championship in the conformation ring are known as Dual Champions; this is extremely prestigious, as it shows that the dog is the ideal blend of form and function, excelling in both areas.

Retriever field trials, designed to simulate "an ordinary day's shoot," are popular and likely the most demanding of these trials. Dogs must "mark" the location of downed feathered game and then return the birds to the shooter. Successful dogs are able to "mark" the downed game by

The beeper on the dog's collar is an alternative to the bell: it helps the hunter follow his Pointer in the field. The hunter can set the beeper to sound every 5 to 20 seconds, depending on the thickness of the cover. When the dog points the game, the beeper stops or emits a steady sound, depending on the setting.

dog's ability to perform his breed's original purpose in the field. The events vary depending on the type of dog, but in all trials dogs compete against one another for placement and for points toward their Field Champion (FC) titles. Dogs that earn their FC titles plus their

remembering where the bird fell as well as correct use of the wind and terrain. Dogs are tested both on land and in water.

Difficulty levels are based on the number of birds downed as well as the number of "blind retrieves" (where a bird is placed away from the view of the dog and the handler directs the dog by the use of hand signals and verbal commands). The term "Non-Slip" retriever, often applied to these trials, refers to a dog that is steady at the handler's side until commanded to go. Every field trial includes four stakes of increasing levels of difficulty. Each stake is judged by a team of two judges who look for many natural abilities, including steadiness, courage, style, control and training.

Field trials sponsored by UKC can either be wild bird trials (Type W) or liberated bird trials (Type L), in which birds are shot and must be retrieved by the dogs. Dogs are evaluated against other dogs in these competitive events. Placing in both types of trials is required to earn the Champion of the Field (CHF) title.

HUNTING TESTS

Hunting tests are not competitive like field trials, and participating dogs are judged against a standard, as in a conformation show. The first hunting tests were devised by the North

American Hunting Retriever Association (NAHRA) as an alternative to field trials for retriever owners to appreciate their dogs' natural innate ability in the field without the expense and pressure of a formal field trial. The intent of hunting tests is the same as that of field trials: to test the dog's ability in a simulated hunting scenario.

The AKC instituted its hunting tests in June 1985; since then, their popularity has grown tremendously. The AKC offers three titles at hunting tests, Junior Hunter (JH), Senior Hunter (SH) and Master Hunter (MH). Each title requires that the dog earn qualifying "legs" at the tests: the JH requiring four; the SH, five; and the MH, six. In addition to the AKC, the United Kennel Club also offers hunting tests through its affiliate club, the Hunting Retriever Club, Inc. (HRC), which began the tests in 1984.

UKC POINTING DOG PROGRAM

The UKC offers a Pointing Dog Program that is based on European-style hunting events, combining elements of field trials and hunt tests. These walking trials are aimed at companion bird dogs and are essentially non-competitive, nurturing an atmosphere of good sportsmanship and learning. Hunters and their dogs are encouraged to participate in these rewarding events.

All pointing breeds are evaluated according to breed type. There are two divisions: Novice and Open, and professional handlers are only permitted if they are handling their own dogs. Novice dogs run in solo heats and are not required to be steady to wing and shot. Dogs in the Open division may be run in braces (pairs). Dogs up to three years of age are rewarded for natural ability and receive certificates.

Hunting tests attract the more casual sportsman, as they are not competitive performance events.

INDEX

Page numbers in **boldface** indicate illustrations.

My Pointer

PUT YOUR PUPPY'S FIRST PICTURE HERE

Dog's Name _____

Date _____ Photographer _____